"Every theater artist who follows Jesus will want this book of stories and wisdom in his or her library, but bystanders of either theater or the Christian faith will also treasure getting this peek behind the scenes."

—**Jeff Barker**, Co-author of *Performing the Plays of the Bible*

"Readers will love Richard Young's short devotional essays—probably prescribed to be read once per week. And then they will read it again . . . and again. Young's stories and insights on the integration of Christian faith and performance art will substantially feed the soul of each reader. Young's scriptural applications and prayers will graciously provoke intrapersonal, interpersonal, and group discussions. This is clearly a jewel of an offering for deepening our understanding of how faith informs art and artistic processes!"

—**Paul D. Patton**, Professor Emeritus of Communication and Theater, Spring Arbor University

"Like Jesus himself, Richard does what the best theologians *should* do: he lets the stories of our specific human endeavors identify their own spiritual truths. Career practitioners and theater enthusiasts alike will surely recognize something of themselves in these stories culled from Richard's years of practicing and teaching the craft. The surprise comes when he deftly mines theological insights from these lived moments, prompting second and third glances at both unique and everyday encounters in the theater. The fact that he does this with humor, warmth, and humility is just a bonus."

—**Barrett Hileman**, Associate Professor of Theater, Ambrose University, Calgary, AB

"This book is a much-needed oasis in the desert of ambition and ego that so often occupies vast territories in the theater world. This book invites you to stop, look and listen: *to stop* the hard charging urge to 'get it all done no matter what!'; *to look* at the people and circumstances around you; and *to listen* to the tender whispering of Jesus as He leads you to a deeper love of Him and a deeper appreciation of those around you. If you are a professional or part-time amateur in theater, you will find this book both helpful and precious. I recommend this book to you. Read it. Meditate on the prayers and Scriptures given at the end of each devotional. Your life will be richer for it."

—**Charlie Jones**, Founder of Peculiar People Touring Theater Company and President of Joyful Community, a nonprofit organization dedicated to bridge-building and community enhancement

And the Word Became Flesh

Devotionals for Theater Artists

RICHARD T. YOUNG

Integratio Press

AND THE WORD BECAME FLESH
Devotionals for Theater Artists

Copyright © 2023 by Richard T. Young. All rights reserved. Except for brief quotations in critical publications or reviews, no part of this book may be reproduced in any manner without prior written permission from the publisher. Write: Permissions, Integratio Press, 11503 Easton Dr., Pasco WA, 99301.

An Imprint of Christianity and Communication Studies Network
11503 Easton Dr.
Pasco, WA 99301

www.theccsn.com

Cover design: Carol O'Callaghan and Mandi Voegele
Interior design: Mary Bryant
Image: Depositphotos

paperback isbn: 978-0-9991463-7-8
ebook isbn: 978-0-9991463-8-5

Integratio Press

All Scripture verses quoted here are from the public domain *World English Bible*.

All the incidents described are real and actually happened. All the names have been changed.

Library of Congress Control Number: 2022948082

Dedication

For Carol Ann, who left this world too early. She put up with being alone for so many long evenings while I was away at rehearsal. I frequently ended my program director's notes with "Carol Ann, I'll be home soon." That remains true.

Table of Contents

Acknowledgements	xiii
About the Author	xv

Devotionals

1.	Hiding God's Word . . . Under My Costume Sleeve	1
2.	Whose Desire?	3
3.	Stage Worship	5
4.	Soul-knowing	7
5.	Say What?	9
6.	Don't Be a Donkey Unless You Sound Like One	11
7.	You Slapped Who?	13
8.	A Line, a Line, My Kingdom for a Line	15
9.	Um . . . What Do I Do Now?	17
10.	Is Anybody There?	19
11.	Closing the Gap	21
12.	Speaking Slowly, Speaking Well	23
13.	Risk Big, Risk Wisely	25
14.	Failing and Falling Leaders	27
15.	Words Make a Difference	29
16.	Holding Down a Corner . . . Not	31
17.	All in the Family	33
18.	God's Will . . . Is in the Trash	35
19.	Missing the Holy Spirit	37
20.	What Key?	39

Table of Contents

21.	The Little Things Count	41
22.	Speaking the Truth . . . in Love	43
23.	Context Is Everything	45
24.	Ready or Not	47
25.	Ummm . . . This Is Not Working	49
26.	Putting Flesh on the Words	51
27.	It's Your Line!	53
28.	Being You . . . Being Them	55
29.	Love or Law	57
30.	What Is Acting?	59
31.	Learning to Hide the Truth in Our Hearts	61
32.	A Mind in Neutral	63
33.	Adlibbing Truth	65
34.	I Am His	67
35.	Why Don't You Tell Them about That!	69
36.	How Did I Do That?	71
37.	Who Wrote This?	73
38.	Unbalanced	75
39.	A Group Effort	77
40.	His Approval	79
41.	That's How He Wrote It	81
42.	I Had All the Fun	83
43.	What Time Does the Show Start . . . Really?	85
44.	Finding God's Kingdom	87
45.	The Most Beautiful Thing I've Seen All Day	89
46.	What Lives On?	91
47.	What Does It Mean to Be Christian, If Not This?	93
48.	Do the Work and Trust God to Provide	95
49.	Fear or Respect?	97
50.	To Be or Not To Be	99
51.	Quantity Versus Quality	101
52.	To Achieve Quality . . .	103

TABLE OF CONTENTS

53. Of Arrogance and Humility	105
54. Don't Do It!	107
Endnotes	111
Scripture Index	113
Subject Matter Index	115

Acknowledgements

I WANT TO ACKNOWLEDGE my parents, Richard and Shirley Young. They are the key contributors to my life and accomplishments. I was influenced by many wonderful teachers, including Marilyn Bogess, Edward Emanuel, Brian Reeder, and Thomas Hird. I have explored the world of theater with many great colleagues, including Jeff Barker, Barbara Clark, Jeff Taylor, Don Hunter, Karen Pajor, Paul Patton, and Steve Pedersen. I also thank Robert H. Woods Jr. and Integratio Press for giving me this opportunity. Most of all, I want to thank my wife, Carol Ann, for all the late nights she spent alone while I was at rehearsal and for loving me throughout it all.

About the Author

RICHARD T. YOUNG found theater in high school when he followed a cute girl into a drama club meeting (he fell in love, and not just with her). Richard earned his BA in Theater from California State University, Hayward, his MA in Theater from California State University, Fresno, and his MFA in Directing from Lindenwood University. Professor Young has taught theater at Greenville University, Blackburn College, and Bethel University in Indiana. He was a member of and director for Lamb's Players Theater in California. He was co-founder and artistic director of the Summer Repertory Theater at Blackburn College. His plays have been published by I. E. Clark, Dramatic Publishing, and Eldridge Publishing. His play *Bread for Their Mouths, Fire for Their Souls* won the 2017 Searchlight Theater playwriting competition.

1

Hiding God's Word . . . Under My Costume Sleeve

TEN-YEAR-OLD SALLY WAS PLAYING SNOOPY in a full-blown production of *You're a Good Man, Charlie Brown*. No junior version here. She was doing more than a great job. She had natural comic timing, and as an already trained and creative dancer, her rendition of Snoopy's solo song "Supper Time" was a showstopper. But as we got closer and closer to opening night she seemed more and more nervous.

I was a touch mystified, as even at the age of ten she was a seasoned performer. When I asked her about her hesitations, she told me she was worried that she "wouldn't remember." Then I was even more confused, because she knew her lines cold. In fact, she knew everyone's lines. So I prayed with her and was done for the day.

The next day she arrived at dress rehearsal full of confidence. The old Sally was back. I assumed the prayer had done its work. At intermission I complimented her on overcoming her "nerves." I asked her what had changed. She pulled up the sleeve of her costume and there was writing on her arm, but it wasn't her lines. It was the order of the scenes. *You're a Good Man, Charlie Brown* is a series of vignettes. Sally had been worried about forgetting the order of the vignettes. I had to laugh and gave her a big hug. I asked the stage manager to post the order of the scenes a couple of places backstage.

Sally's solution of writing on her arm made me think of how God's Word is supposed to be interwoven into our lives. I recalled the ancient Hebrews, who literally wore God's Word on their heads. I've known more than one Christian theater artist who thought they might try performing one of the Gospels and discovered that as they put God's words to memory, their lives were being radically altered. Such is the power of the Word of God. When we literally make it part of who we are . . . our lives change for the good.

PSALM 119:11
"I have hidden your word in my heart, that I might not sin against you."

PROVERBS 3:3
"Don't let kindness and truth forsake you. Bind them around your neck. Write them on the tablet of your heart."

PRAYER
Jesus, help me to take the time and find the ways to hide your words in my heart and in my head and in my spirit and in my soul. A-men.

PERSONAL NOTES:

2

Whose Desire?

MANY YEARS LATER I can still remember what the ground looked like as I stared at it. I'd been walking to a college theater rehearsal, and a thought went through my mind that stopped me cold in my tracks. That thought put the two most joyous aspects of my life into stark juxtaposition, and it scared me. The thought was this: "What if God calls me *out* of theater?"

Suddenly I was terrified. I'd only discovered theater my senior year of high school when I followed a cute girl into a drama club meeting. (I fell in love, and not just with her.) And although I'd been a Christian since the age of 13, I was just starting to grapple with what it meant for Jesus to be *Lord* of my life. (Thank you, InterVarsity Christian Fellowship.) I don't recall how long I stared at the ground, but I didn't commit the unforgiveable sin of being late to rehearsal. It was, however, very hard to concentrate on rehearsal that night.

Give up theater for Jesus? No, no, no, no. But I knew if He called me to do that . . . I would. My heart sank and sank and sank as I thought about that possibility. I haven't always been the wisest person, but I think my next course of action was a gift of wisdom from the Holy Spirit. I prayed, I searched the Scriptures, and most importantly of all, I talked to the people I thought of as my spiritual mentors.

Along the way I ran across Psalm 37:4 and learned what it really means. Psalm 37:4 doesn't mean that whatever you desire in your heart God will give you. It means that when we delight in God, when we are abiding in Him, then the desires in our heart will be put there by His hand.

One of my mentors challenged me to think of a place in the Bible where God called someone out of something. My quick response was that the Bible is filled with stories about people finding God's call on their lives to be the cause of major life changes. My mentor didn't argue with me. Instead, he repeated the question, "Can you think of a Bible story wherein God calls someone out of something?" I got the point. God doesn't call people *out of* things, He calls people *to* things. Nowhere in the Bible does God tap a person on the shoulder and say, "Hey, you need to stop being a shepherd!" But he does tap people and say, "You need to go be my voice to Pharaoh."

God will never call me out of theater. But if I stay close to Jesus, I might be called to something else. If that happens, I'll go willingly. After all, at that point, it will be the desire of my heart.

PSALM 37:4
"Also delight yourself in Yahweh, and he will give you the desires of your heart."

PRAYER
Jesus, help me to delight in you so that the desires of your heart will be mine, as well. A-men.

PERSONAL NOTES:

3

Stage Worship

I HAD THE FUN OF TEACHING A CLASS called "Theater and Christian Worldview." As a 400-level course, it was taken by college juniors and seniors. These were students who had poured themselves into the theater arts with the goal of continuing to do so for their professional lives. These were also students who had been Christians for a long time. Basic Christian theology wasn't new to them.

One day I brought to class a list of union rules for theater artists. It included all the things about being on time and learning lines and sticking to the director's vision, etc. It was a list of do's and don'ts that, if followed in detail, caused one to devote herself wholeheartedly to the pursuit of theater. My students liked it. While our departmental standards were seriously high, these standards seemed higher, and they thought we should adopt them as our own. And rightly so. To create quality theater, there must be quality commitment by all concerned.

I asked the question, "How would you describe the relationship between someone and something wherein that someone has this kind of day-in and day-out response to that thing?" As we talked, words like "devotion" and "commitment" were used. Finally, one young lady who had been quiet for most of the discussion said, "It's worship. To have your life so fully focused on one activity is an act of worship." (I so very much like it when my students get to the point before I do.) Some of her classmates weren't so sure. Isn't it a kind of blasphemy to worship something other than God?

Then we talked about worship. Is worship what we do or what we feel in our heart or what we say or . . . ? The inevitable conclusion is that what we most fully devote ourselves to doing is what we worship. So does this mean that when I have a 40-hour-or-more-a-week job I'm worshipping my job? It might, but worship is also a function of the heart, mind, and spirit. Who I am and how I behave at work may be the determining factors as to whether I'm worshipping my job or not.

Theater, especially at the professional level, is demanding. But probably no more so than medicine or the law or any number of other professional pursuits. Yet I've known enough theater artists to appreciate that theater can consume you. It can become your whole life. The Christian theater artist must work to find those ways to practice daily worship of the God of the universe, not Thespis and his followers.

Matthew 6:21
". . . for where your treasure is, there your heart will be also."

Prayer
Jesus, make me mindful of worship. Help me to understand what it is that I really worship. Help me to make the focus of my soul the God of all creation. A-men.

Personal Notes:

4

Soul-knowing

WE WERE IN FINAL DRESS for the musical version of *Jane Eyre*, and the first act had rocked the house! Lights went down for act II, the music started, the curtain opened and . . . something was seriously wrong. Here's the "fun" part. I knew something was wrong, but for a long moment I didn't know what it was. Then it hit me. The stage was empty. Instead of the two dozen or so actors who should have been there . . . the stage was bare. The conductor cut the orchestra off. Then, amoebae-like, a swarm of actors scuttled onto the stage. The conductor started the music, and the rest of act II went well.

Two things strike me about that performance. The first is that although I knew something was wrong, I didn't immediately know what was wrong. When we sin against a fellow human being, I'm reasonably sure we know it right away. But I'm not so sure that instant awareness is true when our sin is just between ourselves and God.

The second is this. When I debriefed the incident with my stage managers, I think someone took the blame who was actually innocent. I was still a new faculty to them. They may not have figured out that I'd extend grace to the "culprit," and so I think one of the upper-class members protected a freshman.

The takeaway here is also two things: First, knowing God is an "always" kind of thing. We need to be in touch with our spirit, aware of the condition of our soul. When our sin is just between ourselves and God, we need to know. Frankly, when it dawns on you that something is wrong and that the something is a sin just between yourself and God, you should take that as a good sign. Your spiritual life is on the move in a good way.

Second, while there are circumstances where it may not be a good choice (criminal activity, etc.), when you as a Christian have the opportunity to extend grace . . . do it.

PROVERBS 3:5-6
"Trust in Yahweh with all your heart, and don't lean on your own understanding. In all your ways acknowledge him, and he will make your paths straight."

ISAIAH 41:10
"Don't you be afraid, for I am with you. Don't be dismayed, for I am your God. I will strengthen you. Yes, I will help you. Yes, I will uphold you with the right hand of my righteousness."

PRAYER
Jesus, keep my soul in tune with yours so that I will not sin. When I do sin against you, prick my heart so that it may be healed by your forgiveness and grace. A-men.

PERSONAL NOTES:

5

Say What?

IT WAS A SUMMER THEATER PRODUCTION of *Honk*, and it was most assuredly a family affair. Between the cast and crew, we literally had whole families involved in the production. It was final dress rehearsal, and all was well. I was excited for opening night the next day. Suddenly everything stopped. After a set change in act II . . . nothing happened. No actors came on stage. It all just stopped. I waited a full minute before I leaned into my "god mic" and said, "I don't remember this part from rehearsal!" Of course, I pride myself in not being the angry director, and I thought I did pretty well keeping my displeasure in check. We figured out the problem and moved on.

Later I overheard a couple of dads who were serving as backstage crew. They didn't know I was within earshot of them. They were referring to the pause in act II. The first dad said, "He was pretty mad, wasn't he?" and the second dad replied, "Yeah, and he had good reason to be. But he didn't yell at anyone." Wow! I took it as a great compliment.

There have been plenty of times when as a director I've had to deal with the failures of others that have hurt the production. But only once early on in my career did I yell at a cast and crew. At that time my faculty mentor intervened, pulled me aside, and told me I was acting like the biblical term for a donkey. And he was right. Angry yelling has no place in rehearsal.

The Word Became Flesh

Proverbs 12:18
"There is one who speaks rashly like the piercing of a sword, but the tongue of the wise heals."

Prayer
Lord, help me to keep my tongue in check at all times. A-men.

Personal Notes:

6

Don't Be a Donkey Unless You Sound Like One

As is my custom, I asked Laura, one of my director colleagues, to attend a dress rehearsal of *Midsummer Night's Dream* for the purpose of giving feedback. The feedback would be to me only, not to the cast and crew. She enjoyed the production and had a couple good comments, but most pointedly she noted that after Bottom turned into a donkey he didn't change the way he sounded. Shouldn't he sound like a donkey? Yes, yes, yes! Neither I nor my assistant director nor my stage manager nor the actor himself had thought of that. We all missed it.

I teach my acting/directing students that there are only two things I am sure about when it comes to creating theater. The first is to learn to trust one's own judgment. And the second is to invite people whose judgment you trust to come see your work and give you feedback. Besides the example above, I could give you dozens of examples wherein invited feedback from a colleague resulted in a better production. Sure, there have been lots of thoughts and suggestions that I didn't agree with or incorporate, but the good ideas have always outweighed the bad. And shouldn't our spiritual lives be the same way?

Over the years I've had multiple spiritual mentors, and I covet their thoughts about my spiritual growth. Some of those mentors have been younger but wiser people. It is a mistake to try to grow one's walk with Christ in the isolation of the inner self. Don't grow your life in Christ on your own. Find people whose judgment you trust and seek out their thoughts and observations on your spiritual life. Sometimes their thoughts, suggestions, and comments won't seem right for you. But when they do offer God's wisdom, it will ring as truth in your soul.

PROVERBS 12:15
"The way of a fool is right in his own eyes, but he who is wise listens to counsel."

PRAYER
Lord, bring to my life those whose wise counsel I may trust and grow from each day. A-men.

PERSONAL NOTES:

7

You Slapped Who?

IT WAS ONE OF THE MORE astounding theater moments of my life, and I can still feel the emotions of the moment as I write these words. I took one simple action: I gave someone a well-choreographed stage slap, and the whole audience gasped in unison. I can't say for sure, but I think some of the audience even jumped in their seats.

I was playing a pharisee in an Easter pageant. I stood facing the audience. One step below me with his back to the audience was an actor playing Jesus. One step below him, also with backs to the audience, were two more actors, playing Roman soldiers. It was a seriously well-constructed moment of stage combat. I got a good windup, there was a resounding smack, and Jesus literally flew into the arms of the two soldiers behind him. No one was hurt, but it looked and sounded absolutely real. (Yes, it is possible to do that safely with a talented, well trained fight director on hand.) Yeah, I slapped Jesus. It was all play acting, but the reaction of the audience was astounding. To see anyone, much less Jesus, get smacked that way right before your eyes is disturbing.

Fast-forward to a few years later and my good friend James is preaching. I have to confess: I don't recall his text or his examples or much of what he said, but he managed to touch my heart and soul that day in a way they had never been touched before. He convinced me that my sin hurts God. Sure, I'd always believed that sin is bad, sin is wrong, sin hurts me, sin breaks God's law . . . But hurt God? No, that can't be possible. Can it?

The Word Became Flesh

Yeah, it can. And it does. Our angry words, selfish thoughts, uncharitable actions—all of it. Our sin hurts Him. We slap Jesus constantly. And every time it happens, our souls should gasp and jump.

Ephesians 4:30
"Don't grieve the Holy Spirit of God, in whom you were sealed for the day of redemption."

Prayer
Jesus, help me to treat sin like you did, and say "no" to it every time. A-men.

Personal Notes:

8

A Line, a Line, My Kingdom for a Line

YOU KNOW THE ADAGE that to perform well, one must rehearse well? The opposite is also surely true. To perform poorly, you must rehearse poorly. And we had. I'd been pulled in to replace a cast member who had dropped out only three rehearsals before performance. It was a small part with a few lines, and I figured I could just toss it off. It might even be fun. Fast-forward to the first performance. I had the actor's nightmare come true. I'd been given my cue, I knew it was my time to speak . . . and I didn't have a clue as to what my line was. I drew an absolutely complete blank. You can't get more blank than I was at that moment.

I think I am sometimes blank when it comes to speaking about my faith. I don't believe in sticking my faith in the face of everyone I know or meet, but more than once in my life I could have spoken up in favor of my faith and I didn't. I don't hesitate to talk about my hobbies, my family, my profession, or nearly any other thing about myself. But sometimes I've taken the misstep of not speaking up about my faith. I go blank . . . when actually I have plenty to say.

How does one get to the point where talking about Jesus is as natural as talking about any other part of life? I think some of the answer to that is to "rehearse well," meaning to do the things it takes to stay close to Jesus. Read the Word. Study the Word. Memorize and meditate on the Word. Talk to Jesus. Spend time with other believers talking about your faith. And then someday, when you get the cue, you'll know what to say.

JOHN 14:10
"Don't you believe that I am in the Father, and the Father in me? The words that I tell you, I speak not from myself; but the Father who lives in me does his works."

PRAYER
Lord, help me to speak of you with caring, confident love. A-men.

PERSONAL NOTES:

9

Um . . . What Do I Do Now?

THE LIGHTS CAME UP. I was standing mid-stage with a chair in my hand. No big deal—except that I was supposed to be empty-handed, on the phone, in the middle of a phone call. No big deal—except that it was my very first moment on stage in a play with an audience. Yikes! As I recall, I paused, put the chair down, sort of dialed the phone as I picked it up, and started speaking to whoever was supposed to be on the other end of the phone call from the middle of a sentence. I just did the best I could. My loving but tough high school theater teacher never said a word. So I took that as a good sign.

Sometimes life throws stuff at you that you don't expect and don't know what to do about. I think of the time I was in a friend's car and realized that the friends of my friend were in the back seat smoking marijuana. Or when my father died unexpectedly in his fifties. Or when my dorm room was suddenly occupied by a third person, who was female, who was in bed with my roommate. Or when my Pentecostal friends weren't sure I was a Christian because I didn't speak in tongues. Or when my heart was broken for the first time, or the thirtieth time or . . . The list could be a long one.

The funny thing here is that when really bad things happen, things we don't expect and don't know what to do about, we cry out to God: Why did this happen? How could God let this happen? But when really good things happen . . . we don't. No one ever gets offered their dream job and then goes to their prayer closet saying, "God! Why did this happen?" When the person you've been in love with since the fifth grade agrees to marry you, asking God "Why?" doesn't usually follow.

I think our responses in all those situations, both good and bad, are a measure of how well we "abide" in Jesus. Two of the synonyms for "abide" are "live" and "dwell." When my life throws me into the unexpected, if I have been dwelling in the Lord of the universe, then at the very least I know I'm going to have some help along the way.

John 14:4–5
"Remain in me, and I in you. As the branch can't bear fruit by itself, unless it remains in the vine, so neither can you, unless you remain in me. I am the vine. You are the branches. He who remains in me, and I in him, the same bears much fruit, for apart from me you can do nothing."

Prayer
Lord, help me to accept that there will always be life complications, both good and bad. Teach me to abide in you always that I may bring your truth to all of life. A-men.

Personal Notes:

10

Is Anybody There?

IT WAS THE UNMISTAKABLE VOICE of our stage manager, and she was angry. "Is anybody there?" sounded again from our booth monitor. (This was in the days before headsets.) "Um, yes," I replied. "I'm sorry. I know we missed that cue. Could we run it again please?" See, the thing was we hadn't just missed a cue, we had missed a cue *again*! My buddy and I were running the lights for a community theater production of *A Lion in Winter*.

This was also in the days before computer-controlled light boards. Even though there were only a handful of light cues, it took both of us to turn all the knobs and pull all the levers needed to affect a lighting change.

The local amateur cast was doing a great job of bringing the tale to life, and even from the booth we were getting caught up in the illusion. The cue in question was at the end of a scene. The mother and one of her wayward adult sons were on stage having just ended a powerful and intimate conversation. He was kneeling at her feet with his head in her lap. They spoke the last line and waited for the lights to fade, and waited, and waited and ... We missed it once and were given a "talking to" by the stage manager. This was now the second time we'd missed it, and she was angry. There was no reason to have missed this cue, save for our lack of attention.

They backed up the scene a page or two and started again. This time I stood up, and even raised one foot off the floor. It's an old concentration trick. If my foot drops, it is a cue that I have lost focus on what I am supposed to be doing. We got to the end of the scene, and the light fade was a thing of beauty. Our monitor squawked again, but instead of the high praise I'd hoped for our stage manager said, "That was better. Let's do it again. Frank [the director] wants one more second off the fade." And we ran it again, and then, just to be sure, again and again.

It is so easy to become complacent and not focused on my walk with Christ, especially when my life is in good shape. And fortunately for me, most of the time, my life has been in good shape. Sure, I've had my bouts with sin and tragedy and depression, but overall it's been a good life. As noted before in these devotions, when our lives are in turmoil we throw ourselves at Christ's feet. Why don't we do that when our lives are in great shape?

I've been trying to lose weight. The problem is that when I've lost a few pounds, I tend to get lax on my diet. I've learned that when I have lost a few pounds, it is not the time to celebrate. It is instead the time to dig in and keep at it. I need to do the same kind of thing in my walk with Christ. When my life is going well is when I should dig into those things that bring me closer to Him. When I can say "My life ROCKS!" is when I should make sure I am daily focused on Him who is the Rock.

1 PETER 5:8
"Be sober and self-controlled. Be watchful. Your adversary, the devil, walks around like a roaring lion, seeking whom he may devour."

PRAYER
Help me to be alert in you. After all, the world needs more "lerts." A-men. (I hope God has a good sense of humor. If He doesn't I am in *huge* trouble.)

PERSONAL NOTES:

11

Closing the Gap

I'D LET THE ACTORS AND CREW GO. We'd had our notes, and it was time (11:00 p.m. or later) for everyone to go home and rest. But one of the notes I'd given was to the sound operator/stage manager. It was tech week, and we'd run one of the sound cues five times without getting it right.

I'd had the sound operator/stage manager stay late with me to run that cue again and again . . . to get it right. "Right" in this context meant meeting my artistic judgment. There was an exact moment when the sound cue would "work" artistically, and we hadn't achieved that yet. The young lady who was working the cue from the booth was intelligent and capable. The problem was one of communication. With me in the house trying to describe to her what I wanted, it just hadn't worked.

I joined her in the booth, and between the two of us we had quickly been able to make the cue work exactly as I wanted. The change in proximity was all it took to solve the communication glitch.

And aren't we like that in our walk with God? It's up to us to stay close to God. God is always with us. If there is some "felt" distance, it's because we have moved. When we ignore or don't pursue our goal of abiding in Christ . . . we don't. Our proximity to God is up to us. God is always available. The Holy Spirit is encamped in our hearts. We ignore that to our own misfortune. If we want our lives to "work," then we have to work to stay close to the Lord of the cosmos.

James 4:8
"Draw near to God, and he will draw near to you."

Prayer
Jesus, remind me daily that I need to BE with you. A-men.

Personal Notes:

12

Speaking Slowly, Speaking Well

SARAH WAS IN HER EARLY 20S, and she needed to look like she was 80 or more. She was playing the grandmother in *Lost in Yonkers* and was, as they say, crushing it. We were having trouble finding the right makeup to give her that truly aged look. Our talented makeup designer tried a process by which Sarah's whole face was covered with wet latex that when dried gave her all the wrinkles of a prune. It worked really well. But to my chagrin, when the makeup designer first presented a "latexed-up" Sarah to me I said, "I hate it!" It was the wrong thing for a director to say at that moment, and I spent the next hour apologizing to my makeup designer.

The Book of Proverbs has a lot to say about our use of the tongue to create the spoken word, and I think I violated every one of those cautions in that moment.

The old adage to engage one's brain before opening one's mouth is, in many ways, scriptural. Words have power. We all know what a crock that old saying is: "Sticks and stones may break my bones, but words will never hurt me." Words can hurt in a mighty way. The words spoken to a child form the person he or she becomes. The words we use in our own minds to describe ourselves to ourselves are extremely powerful. Theater, too, is all about words. We take the words on the page and bring them to life.

How much better it would have been if I'd paused, thought about my response, and said something like, "Hmmm, this doesn't strike me well, but let's look at it under the lights."

Ephesians 4:29

"Let no corrupt speech proceed out of your mouth, but only what is good for building others up as the need may be, that it may give grace to those who hear."

Prayer

Lord, please bless me with the ability to tame my tongue and speak well in all circumstances. A-men.

Personal Notes:

13

Risk Big, Risk Wisely

The audience was excited, full of anticipation! The set was all glass and mirrors, and it was rumored that there was a rock and roll band to underscore the aged text with new music. The play in question was a somewhat gruesome but revered piece, and this director had made seriously interesting choices. The costumes were all chains and leather, and the characterizations spoke of pop culture, punk rock, and some in-your-face theater. It was also rumored that the set would . . . bleed!

The house lights dimmed, the curtain opened, and . . . not long into act I, the audience was laughing at stuff that wasn't supposed to be funny. In simple terms, it was a huge disaster.

Given the nature of this festival, we knew that a couple of knowledgeable people would be making a verbal response to this production the next morning. I couldn't imagine what the respondents would say. That morning the auditorium was packed. I wasn't the only one wondering what could be said.

I don't recall the name of the man who started the response, but I can still see his face. It seemed like he wasn't sure what to say either, but that turned out to be a false impression. He made a couple of opening remarks welcoming everyone and acknowledging the cast and crew. Then he started in. He recognized that the play hadn't received the response the cast and crew were hoping for; he knew that things had gone terribly wrong. Then he switched gears and noted that he had to commend them highly for at least one thing.

I couldn't imagine what that could be. Then he talked about the people who created *Cats* and those who created *Starlight Express* and how easily those projects could have failed miserably. He talked about some successful Broadway producers and some of the failures those producers had experienced. He went on with, "I have to highly commend and compliment those who had the artistic vision for this production. You risked big-time, and we can't have amazing, astounding life-changing theater without taking big risks."

When the risk is big, the win can be big. But it can also fail big. One must risk wisely, but one must risk.

The Bible is filled with people who were called on by God to take a big risk. Simply being a Christian dedicated to the theater arts is a risk. Professional theater is a tough world to make your way into.

Challenges to your faith and demands to compromise on what you believe are everywhere in the theater world. But risk wisely. It's important to be sure that theater IS God's call on your life. Once you are confident in that . . . forge ahead.

MATTHEW 14:29
"He said, 'Come!' Peter stepped down from the boat, and walked on the waters to come to Jesus."

2 TIMOTHY 1:7
"For God didn't give us a spirit of fear, but of power, love, and self-control."

PRAYER
Lord, I thank you for your call on my life. Help me to hear your voice clearly, discern my call well, and be willing and able to risk wisely for you. A-men.

PERSONAL NOTES:

14

Failing and Falling Leaders

My wife, Carol Ann, and I decided to go to Memphis one summer to see the National Civil Rights Museum. Upon arrival I checked the local theaters to see what was playing and delightfully discovered that a famous older male vocalist was appearing in a production of *Camelot* at the wonderful Orpheum Theater. This was a double serendipity. A well-known performer that we'd not seen before in a classic old theater space. What's not to like?

We settled in our seats, the lights went down, the curtain went up and . . . we were instantly disappointed. I was tempted to walk out. This well-known performer wasn't even trying. I suspect he was a touch drunk. In the hiding-in-the-tree scene he literally fell out of the tree. The only reason we stayed is because the rest of the cast members were performing their hearts out trying to save the show.

I felt sorry for them.

The sad commentary here is that this kind of thing happens too often in the Christian community, as well. I knew a man who went to work for a world-class Christian organization only to find himself under a boss who didn't believe in change. The boss came from a culture where the ideas from those supervised weren't supposed to be proposed. The boss came from a culture where the patriarch was always right without question. This man I knew did the best he could in those circumstances: he prayed and waited for a new direction. It eventually came from within the same organization, and he moved on to a more fulfilling ministry. The leader in that instance eventually was removed from that position and then proceeded to sue the organization.

How does a Christian deal with subservience to those who don't lead well? Are we simply supposed to believe that God has called our Christian leaders to their places and that we must trust in that? I know a person who thought he was up for a big promotion at a Christian organization and didn't get it. Nonetheless he told the leaders he knew he was under their "umbrella of leadership and trusted in that." And in his circumstance, I think he was right. The leaders in that instance were wise, caring people who had sought God's guidance and made as wise a choice as they could make.

Ultimately, we are serving God and must seek Him in all circumstances, including those in which our worldly leaders are failing us. There is no easy answer here, save that by abiding in Christ, listening carefully and wisely for God's voice, and seeking His face we will eventually find direction.

1 Thessalonians 5:12–13
"But we beg you, brothers, to know those who labor among you, and are over you in the Lord, and admonish you, and to respect and honor them in love for their work's sake. Be at peace among yourselves."

Philippians 2:3
"... doing nothing through rivalry or through conceit, but in humility, each counting others better than himself."

Prayer
I ask for those to whom I am subservient, that you would grant them great wisdom and your guidance in all things. And I ask for myself that you would help me to follow and lead according to your will. A-men.

Personal Notes:

15

Words Make a Difference

AS A PLAYWRIGHT, that moment when the house lights go down and the curtain opens is a mixture of terror and joy, especially when you've put your script in the hands of a director whose work you don't really know. I'd submitted a short play called *Of Soldiers and Priests* to a theater company that specialized in producing new works. Pleased that it was chosen for production, I marked my calendar and was there on opening night. They did a decent job with it but had changed a few words in the script that I thought were poor choices.

One character, a young man, had originally referred to a woman's "chest," and they had changed it to "boobs." The character in question was planning to be a priest, so the change did make a difference in the audience's perception of that character. After the show I found the director and made my query, pointing out how the change reflected differently on the nature of the character. The only response I got from the director was something about expecting that directors will make some changes.

As a director, I too have made changes in texts. I've taken out a lot of profanity, especially in situations where the producing organization expected or required it. In most of those cases the differences it made in characterization were minimal, but in one instance I had to work hard as a director to make the character work without the profanity.

This type of change does violate the royalty contract. I've played the game of sending in the royalty check with the unsigned contract knowing that I'd make some very minimal changes. No publishing company has ever called to ask about the unsigned contract, but every one of them has cashed the check. The few times that I've wanted to make a big change, I've queried the publisher, was always denied, and I abided by the denial.

Words have power. John makes that clear at the start of his Gospel. Jesus was God's Word made flesh to bring us the most important message in the universe. The words we choose to use day-in and day-out make a difference in our lives and the lives of others.

A big part of being a theater artist is all about learning to use words well. The words we use to tell stories on stage, the words we use with colleagues as we work to put those stories on stage, the words we use to describe the work of those around us... and the list goes on, all make a difference.

EPHESIANS 4:29
"Let no corrupt speech proceed out of your mouth, but only what is good for building others up as the need may be, that it may give grace to those who hear."

PRAYER
Lord Jesus, inspire me to take account of every word that issues forth from my heart, my mind, my mouth, my pen and to seek to make them all pleasing to you. A-men.

PERSONAL NOTES:

16

Holding Down a Corner ... Not

"Why are you standing there?" The question was put to me by Dr. Williams, my director. I was playing the role of Lennox in a college production of *Macbeth*. Sure that I had the correct answer, I said in wonderful director jargon, "I'm holding down this corner to balance the stage picture." In fact, that was at least part of the reason I was there. Dr. Williams gave me one of his famous incredulous looks and said, "So you think Lord Lennox walked into this room, looked around, decided that the space was lop-sided, and stood here to make it all even?"

I didn't have a ready response, and Dr. Williams wasn't going to come to my rescue. He just looked at me. Finally, I blurted out, "It's a tense situation, and Lord Lennox has put himself on guard here in case he needs to protect the king." Dr. Williams smiled, said "Exactly!", and went on about the business of directing. Had I given the right answer? The first answer, while true, had nothing to do with my character's motivation. The second answer did have to do with my character's motivation, and while there were no doubt multiple motivations for Lennox to stand there, which one I chose didn't make a difference to Dr. Williams. He just wanted me as an actor to have a reason for how my character behaved.

More than once over the years Dr. Williams's voice has come back to me: "Why are you standing there?" But the question gets transmogrified into "Why are you a theater artist? How does it matter to God's Kingdom?" What is my real motivation for teaching and creating theater? How does what I do fit into God's purposes in this world? Sometimes those kinds of questions are scary and difficult to answer. But personal integrity requires that I ask them. The Gospel requires that I ask them. Being true to God's calling on my life requires that I ask them.

If I give myself honest answers, I am not always comfortable with the what, why, and how of my being a theater artist, and I have to rethink and restructure some of what I'm doing with my life. This self-evaluation is an ongoing thing. As noted in a previous devotion, the day may come when God calls me out of theater. It hasn't happened yet, and in the meantime I have to be aware of my motives and make sure they align with the purposes of God's Kingdom.

COLOSSIANS 3:23
"And whatever you do, work heartily, as for the Lord, and not for men."

ROMANS 8:28
"We know that all things work together for good for those who love God, to those *who are called according to his purpose.*" [emphasis added]

PRAYER
Lord of the universe, challenge me daily to keep my heart and head in line with the purposes of your Kingdom. Help me to always keep my actions aligned with your heart and mind. A-men.

PERSONAL NOTES:

17

All in the Family

IT WAS MY FIRST paid directing job. I was ecstatic. I'd proposed a production of *The Madwoman of Chaillot* to the board of the local civic theater, and they'd hired me. And when I say "hired me," that is it. As is the case in many small community theaters, the director was responsible for all of it! From play selection to auditions, from set design to construction, from sound and lighting to advertising and box office, I was responsible for it all. (These days I don't think I'd direct again in that kind of circumstance.)

I was ready for the challenge. I had the energy of youth, and I had my family. My dad did the lighting, my mom did the props, my sister helped with costuming, and my brothers ran the lighting and the sound. It was a family affair, and to my chagrin I think I spent all of what I made on my own needs instead of getting some nice gifts for my family. I did see to it that everyone was well recognized in the program notes. Looking back, I know I was fortunate to have them. I could not have produced the show without them.

All of us in theater know it takes a lot of people doing a lot of work to put on a show. One of the reasons I like theater is because of how much a good production company functions like the body of Christ, at least in the sense that everyone has a specific role to play. Without everyone doing their job, the production is incomplete.

I've been around enough theater groups that I know the feeling of family that can come from working on a production together. This family-ness is especially prevalent in educational theater, where one might work on multiple productions over multiple years with many of the same people.

How I do my part in the body of Christ is a reflection of my relationship with God. That reflection can also show up when I function well with my secular theater family. I'm God's child no matter where I am, and I need to behave with grace as my truth, no matter what other family I am surrounded by.

Ephesians 4:15–16
". . . but speaking truth in love, we may grow up in all things into him, who is the head, Christ; from whom all the body, being fitted and knit together through that which every joint supplies, according to the working in measure of each individual part, makes the body increase to the building up of itself in love."

Prayer
Master, guide me into actions that speak of my eternal connection to your family. A-men.

Personal Notes:

18

God's Will . . . Is in the Trash

IT WAS MY FIRST real theater paycheck. The local civic theater had hired me to direct. I made my final report to the board and was handed a check for a relatively nice sum of money. I'd made it. I was getting paid to do theater . . . certainly not enough to give up my day job . . . but still . . .

Even though I really needed the money, I didn't cash the check for several days. Having that check was a validation of my status as a theater artist. Once I'd cashed the check that certification would be gone, and who knew how long it would be before I'd make money as a theater artist again?

My weakening bank account finally mandated the cashing of that check. I'd thought about taking a picture of it, but this was long before smart phones and I didn't have a camera. So I took one last longing look at it and headed for the bank. On my way to the car I took out my trash. I dumped my trash, and then the stuff that had been at the bottom of the pile was on the top of the pile. Right on the very top was a newsletter from a Christian organization I was interested in but couldn't afford to support financially. That's when it occurred to me that I needed to tithe my theater money. I pocketed the newsletter and wrote them a check when I got back from the bank. It felt good to write that check, especially since this was from money I'd earned doing theater.

The Word Became Flesh

1 Peter 2:15
"For this is the will of God, that by well-doing you should put to silence the ignorance of foolish men."

Mark 3:35
"For whoever does the will of God, the same is my brother, and my sister, and mother."

Prayer
Jesus, make me always sensitive to the prodding of your Holy Spirit. Don't let me miss opportunities to do your will because I'm not listening. May serendipities of doing your will color my life daily. A-men.

Personal Notes:

19

Missing the Holy Spirit

I CALLED CHARLIE just to check in and see how he was doing. Charlie is a relatively well-known actor/director, and the serendipities of life had brought him to my campus to direct for us. At this time in his life, cancer had invaded his body. I called to ask about his medical condition but instead got a spiritual report. He told me that he missed working with people who were filled with the Holy Spirit. He'd gone back to his secular institution and was feeling the spiritual emptiness. It occurred to me that Charlie must be incredibly in touch with his spiritual life, with his soul.

How does one get that in touch with one's soul, one's spiritual inner being?

I well recalled his time with us on campus. He was a man of prayer. He didn't just start and end rehearsal with a prayer but prayed his way through the day. One night late after rehearsal, he called a friend at a well-known nearby "religious" university. As all of us were headed to our beds, he was looking for a place to go pray. The next day he spoke in our chapel. It was clear to me that he'd prayed all night. The spiritual responsibility of speaking in chapel had been a motivating factor.

He told about his "Godless" years as a TV actor, how an affair had destroyed his marriage and him along with it. He told about his redemption and new life in Christ. I think it was the first time a television/movie "star" had been a speaker in our chapel. Still, of all the things Charlie ever said to me, his comment about missing the work with people who are filled with the Holy Spirit stands out in my memory.

We need to be a people in touch with the Holy Spirit and in touch with our souls on a moment-to-moment basis. Prayer is clearly a key to that state of being.

1 CORINTHIANS 12:7
"But to each one is given the manifestation of the Spirit for the profit of all."

JOHN 14:26
"But the Counselor, the Holy Spirit, whom the Father will send in my name, he will teach you all things, and will remind you of all that I said to you."

PRAYER
Lord Jesus, prod me into the thoughts and actions that will help me be aware of your Holy Spirit in my daily life. A-men.

PERSONAL NOTES:

20

What Key?

As the production manager for a small Christian theater company, I had the interesting task of training stage managers. We pulled our stage managers from production staff, including actors, who didn't have a big assignment for that particular production. So I trained a lot of stage managers, which included teaching them how to set up and care for props. Standard practice was to make and use a prop "map." At least that is what we called it. We'd cover the prop table with a large piece of brown paper, lay out all the props on it, then draw around each prop and label the image. Once the prop map was completed, the stage manager simply rolled out the map, placed the props on it, and instantly knew if anything was missing.

One night as I made my first act II entrance, I went by the prop table to grab the large key that I was supposed to bring on stage. It wasn't there. I instantly noticed that the prop map wasn't being used. With no time to look for the key, I went on stage, ad-libbed a line to cover for the missing prop, and went on with the show.

After the show it was my job to "deal with" the stage manager. My query to him: "Why didn't you use the prop map?" He answered, "Oh, I know where all the props go." I told him about the missing key, and he unfortunately didn't think it was much of a problem. What if it had been a prop critical to the scene? He didn't stage-manage for us again and left the company soon after.

Over the years, without fail, when a stage manager under my

care gave up using the preshow checklist or the prop map, something went amiss... every time.

Sometimes in our Christian walk we think we know where all the props go, and we miss something. I don't mean to suggest that there are prop maps and preshow checklists one uses to be a Christian. But I do mean to say that anytime we think we can ignore the basics, or simply get complacent in our spiritual life, it's a mistake. No, we don't earn God's grace by going to church or reading our Bible or engaging in prayer on a regular basis, but those things are the water and fertilizer and sunshine of our spiritual well-being. We put them aside to our own detriment.

JAMES 5:13
"Is any among you suffering? Let him pray. Is any cheerful? Let him sing praises."

PSALM 141:2
"Let my prayer be set before you like incense; the lifting up of my hands like the evening sacrifice."

REVELATION 14:7
"He said with a loud voice, 'Fear the Lord, and give him glory; for the hour of his judgment has come. Worship him who made the heaven, the earth, the sea, and the springs of waters!'"

PRAYER
Jesus, prod me when I don't do the things that I know will bring me closer to you. A-men.

PERSONAL NOTES:

21

The Little Things Count

REGGIE WAS A seriously good stage manager. When I saw that she would be my SM for our musical that year, I was pleased. We proceeded as normal, and all went well. But I recall with clarity one rehearsal where I'd reblocked an actor to make the next part of the action simpler. Without that movement the actor had to wind his way around several other actors to get off stage on the next line. Reggie asked, "Why is he moving there?" Reggie knew that if she had questions to ask or ideas to offer, I wanted to hear them. (Not true of all directors.) So I explained about the next action being simpler. "No," Reggie said, "Why is *Hank* [the character's name] moving there?" Ah, yes; the character must have a motivation. Maybe Reggie had seen a touch of confusion on the face of the actor. Reggie was sensitive like that and really took good care of her actors. So I queried the actor, and between the three of us we came up with Hank's reason for moving. Did it make a big difference in the show? No, but it did make a difference in that performer's ability to stay in character and to make that scene work well. Would it have mattered much if Reggie hadn't taken the moment to show concern and ask the question? Probably not. But Reggie had cared well for a fellow artist, and that does matter.

We don't know what we'll say or do that will touch someone in some small way that makes a difference. I remember being shocked when a colleague, a person I'd locked horns with more than once, complimented me on how "humanely" I ran the Humanities

Division after I became chair. Really? I'd made it a practice to send each of the faculty a note of encouragement and thanks at least once a semester. My spiritual gift is encouragement, so it didn't seem like all that big of a deal to me. Apparently it touched my colleague in a significant way.

In theater there are so many ways to be kind and helpful to other people. The extra "thank you," the appreciative smile, the credit where credit is due, the moment of encouragement, the extra effort to get it right every time . . . it all makes an impact, and in your case that impact is in the name of Christ.

PROVERBS 16:24
"Pleasant words are a honeycomb, sweet to the soul, and health to the bones."

COLOSSIANS 4:6
"Let your speech always be with grace, seasoned with salt, that you may know how you ought to answer each one."

HEBREWS 10:24
"Let us consider how to provoke one another to love and good works."

PRAYER
Lord Jesus, infect me with your Holy Spirit, so that contagion-like I may spread you to everyone my life touches. A-men.

PERSONAL NOTES:

22

Speaking the Truth . . . in Love

I WAS THE SCENE CHANGE CAPTAIN for a production of *The Threepenny Opera* that had a huge set. In one scene, six horse stalls flew in just fine, but on the way out something was going wrong. I quickly identified the problem. The student working that batten had gotten confused, and instead of pulling up on the counterweight rope, he was pulling down. This lowered that part of the set and caused it to lean. Then he'd realized his mistake and pulled the correct way, but the set started to wobble on the way up. As I stood watching, it hit another piece, and one of the two wires holding it broke. It was now hanging above the stage swinging around wildly. I yelled "hold," and everything stopped. After a flurry of activity, we got it cut down and off the stage just in time for the curtain to open on the next scene. The rest of the show played without incident.

After the show, a bunch of the tech crew was gathered around the broken piece. As I approached, I could hear the argument. They were clearly trying to figure out who was at fault for this incident. Suddenly Dr. Coch, our director, approached. Dr. Coch was really good at playing the moment. Silently, he looked around at the gathered crew, making eye contact with all of them.

Then in a controlled and calm voice he said, "Really? No one did this on purpose. It doesn't matter whose fault this is. What matters is that we figure out why it happened and how to fix it." That was my cue to speak. "Dr. Coch, may I see you privately for a moment?" I told him what I had observed, and I identified which member of the fly crew was the "confused one."

Later, as I was about to leave the theater, I heard voices coming from what should have been an empty stage. I looked in from a wing. There was Dr. Coch, our technical director, and the fly crew member who had been "confused." Dr. Coch and the TD were giving the student a refresher course in how the fly system worked.

What stays in my mind is that there was no angry yelling, no belittling of that student in front of others, no public condemnation for his mistake. In a quiet, even private, teaching session, the corrections had been made.

Unfortunately, I've more than once seen a theater teacher or director belittle, insult, degrade, disparage, demean, and publicly condemn a cast or crew member for a mistake. I recall reading about an acting teacher who had a reputation for bringing students to tears, and apparently thought that was a good thing. I don't know what those instructors were thinking. That kind of behavior never endears them to their charges.

I suppose some people confuse fear with respect.

Ephesians 4:29
"Let no corrupt speech proceed out of your mouth, but only what is good for building others up as the need may be, that it may give grace to those who hear."

Prayer
Lord, help me to live Ephesians 4:29 every moment of my life. And give me the ability to bring some healing to my colleagues when they have been verbally wounded by an unkind and unloving supervisor. Finally, help me to find ways to love those supervisors in your name. A-men.

Personal Notes:

23

Context Is Everything

I WAS PLAYING ANDY in Neil Simon's uproarious comedy *The Star-Spangled Girl*. I and my two other cast members were seasoned performers, and we had an eight-day, two-weekend run at a small community theater. The houses were packed, and by the second performance, we knew when to hold for laughs. Even better, we knew when the next line would engage a good laugh. I well remember sitting in the middle of the stage, holding for a laugh, waiting to say my next line, confident that it would garner another huge laugh. You'd think that kind of confidence would be based on something seriously clever, but the line was, "That's why they put five sticks in a pack, Norman." It's kind of a mundane, unfunny line. But within the context of the play it was hysterical. Even better, I discovered that my delivery of the line didn't matter much. Regardless of how I said it, the audience laughed.

As Christians called into the theater arts, we are always within two contexts: the world of theater, with all its joy and sorrow, work and play, rejection and confirmation, and the world of our walk with Christ, with all its challenges and triumphs, blessings and failures, assurances and doubts.

As with all Christians, in all walks of life, we are mistaken if we think we can keep these two contexts separate. In fact, we are called to blend them so that our wholeness in Christ calls out to the brokenness of the world saying, "Come be healed!" When called into the world of theater as a life's work, that world becomes the mission field. It is the context wherein we must strive to work out and demonstrate our faith.

I recall James, a fellow cast member in a college production. As with most casts, we got close to each other. Theater is intimate work. Sometimes we had deep discussions, other times we shared our life's joys and sorrows openly. James was a leading-man type who went on after college to make a number of films. James once asked me, "What would you do if you were in love with two women and couldn't decide who to stay with?" I can't say God gave me the words, but I didn't even have to think about my response. "I'd pray about it." James was quiet for a moment, then said, "You are always there, aren't you?" "Where?" I asked. "With God." James continued, "You're all about hanging out with God." I was a touch mystified, since this was the only time I could recall talking to James about spiritual things. God allowed me to bring my context into James's world.

Galatians 1:10

"For am I now seeking the favor of men, or of God? Or am I striving to please men? For if I were still pleasing men, I wouldn't be a servant of Christ."

Prayer

Jesus, make me always mindful that the first and only real context of my life is my walk with you. I want that wholeness to infiltrate everything I do and everything I say. A-men.

Personal Notes:

24

Ready or Not

I REMEMBER THE FIRST TIME I said it. I'd learned the idea from my graduate professor Dr. Theo. His wise counsel was that the goal of rehearsal was to be performance-ready two rehearsals before opening. I don't think I've ever achieved that goal, but I have been performance-ready one rehearsal before opening.

It was our second to last dress rehearsal of a summer production of *Oliver*, and the rehearsals had run well— extremely well. The tech crew hadn't missed a beat. The cast was high energy and in a creative state. The orchestra had crushed it. If we'd had an audience that night, they wouldn't have known it was a rehearsal. We hadn't had to stop for anything.

We gathered for notes, but there weren't very many, and then, looking over my cast, crew, and musicians, I said the nearly unthinkable. "If we had two more rehearsals, I'd cancel one." What? Cancel a rehearsal this close to opening? Are you crazy!?! No, no I'm not. This was community theater. Everyone there had a day job, and doing theater was their volunteer joy. And they hadn't just rehearsed that night, they had *performed*. If it had been possible, an evening off would have been a benefit to all. But alas, we only had one rehearsal left, and I couldn't risk it. The next night's rehearsal was amazing. I'd wished we'd had an audience.

How much do we strive to get our spiritual lives "ready"? We do all those things "Christians" are supposed to do to be "good" Christians. But I wonder if there isn't a director in the wings telling us to cancel the rehearsal. Jesus wants us to be His because *we* want to be His, not because we feel like we *have* to be His. I recently told a friend who had complimented me on my walk with Christ (Wow, where did that come from?), "I just do the best I can, and then I wallow around in a big pile of grace." The bottom line is that no matter how much we prepare, we can't save ourselves. It's all about His grace. I told another friend recently, "I don't think accepting Jesus is so much about heaven and hell as it is about loving Him and wanting to party with Him forever." Yeah, that might sound like heresy to some, but what do I know? . . . I'm just a theater artist.

PHILIPPIANS 1:6
". . . being confident of this very thing, that he who began a good work in you will complete it until the day of Jesus Christ."

PRAYER
Jesus, help me to do my best to be your disciple, but make sure I know that it's your grace that brings me into your arms . . . not my works. A-men.

PERSONAL NOTES:

25

Ummm... This Is Not Working

I DON'T KNOW if this is a universal phenomenon for directors, but I've known enough directors and been in enough rehearsals to suspect that it is something all directors experience. I used to fear it. It was a moment that I didn't want to happen, and I'd do everything I could to avoid it, but it would join me on stage and haunt me nonetheless. Thus, I teach my directing students to expect it.

It goes like this: I'm blocking the show, figuring out where the actors move and stand and why the characters are doing those things. It happens when I have a lot of actors on stage. The rehearsal is moving along well when suddenly I take a pause and realize... this isn't working! Even though I've pre-blocked the action, it just isn't doing justice to the moment. I find myself standing in the middle of the stage, script in hand, not knowing what to do next, and all my actors are waiting on me.

Although I still try to avoid it, I've come to enjoy that moment, even look forward to it.

Directing is creative work. The I-don't-know-what-to-do-next pause forces my creative juices to flow. It tells me I am trying to do my best work. It means the creative, discovery, artistic process of theater is flowing... and I love it. It's a good sign.

I think in our walk with Christ those moments of confusion, uncertainty, and doubt may well be good signs. When I have to struggle with my faith is when I grow in my faith. When I have doubts and questions is when I search and study and learn. When something in my faith walk isn't working is when I ask the hard questions. And if there is anything I am sure of about being a Christian, I know this . . . it is a *mistake* to ignore the hard questions, to pretend they aren't there. God is . . . God. God can handle the tough stuff. And there are a lot of Christian teachers and leaders and authors who will help you find answers to those hard questions. Philip Yancey is one of my favorite Christian writers. His honest approach to faith and hard questions has helped mold my faith in multiple ways. Os Guinness's book on doubt was life-changing for me, as well.[1]

So whether you stumble on stage or stumble in your faith walk . . . celebrate. It's a good sign. But don't let the stumble stop you. Push on.

1 Peter 5: 6–11
"Humble yourselves therefore under the mighty hand of God, that he may exalt you in due time; casting all your worries on him, because he cares for you. Be sober and self-controlled. Be watchful. Your adversary, the devil, walks around like a roaring lion, seeking whom he may devour. Withstand him steadfast in your faith, knowing that your brothers who are in the world are undergoing the same sufferings. But may the God of all grace, who called you to his eternal glory by Christ Jesus, after you have suffered a little while, perfect, establish, strengthen, and settle you. To him be the glory and the power forever and ever. A-men."

Prayer
Lord, Yahweh: In those times when I struggle with my faith, when I'm confronting the hard questions, when I don't know what to do next, help me to fear not! Help me to lean on you and push ahead. Don't let me back down. A-men.

Personal Notes:

26

Putting Flesh on the Words

In *The Empty Space,* theater genius Peter Brook writes about one of his first big directing jobs.[1] He tells how he got a model of the set and had cardboard numbers representing each actor. He tells how he blocked and re-blocked the opening scene, moving all his cardboard actors around the model set, making lots of notes in his script. The big day for the first blocking rehearsal arrived, and Brook set about moving his performers in the ways that he'd orchestrated the cardboard pieces, only to discover the obvious. Actors are far more animated than cardboard pieces. They'd add a bow here and a movement there. Wisely, Brook closed his script and waded in among the actors, never looking back. There on stage with his cast he became one of them and together they created performance. He didn't give up his authority as director, but he recognized the individuality of his cast and their creative efforts. He became one of them.

In the person of Jesus, God waded in among His people. He became one of us. He lived and breathed as we live and breathe. He faced death as we do. He never surrendered His authority over all creation, but He chose to suffer for our sake. He wanted us to know Him.

I've often thought that the first part of John 1:14 is also a description of what we try to do in theater. What Brook did is a worldly illustration of what God did in Jesus. More than once I've been able to make the analogy as I talk about the theories and meanings of theater with non-Christian colleagues. As Christians we should know the place of theater arts within our worldview.

The Word Became Flesh

John 1:14
"The Word became flesh, and lived among us. We saw his glory, such glory as of the one and only Son of the Father, full of grace and truth."

Prayer
Thank you, Lord, for putting on our flesh, for "wading in amongst" us. Help me to learn to live that truth in my theater endeavors. A-men.

Personal Notes:

27

It's Your Line!

"You were given your cue! Why didn't you speak your lines?" Miss Ballard was a demanding director, and it was literally my first moments on stage in the rehearsal of a play. I hadn't spoken my lines because the actor before me hadn't said all of his. He had given me my cue, but he'd left out other stuff.

I started to explain this as the reason for my pause when Miss Ballard overhauled my understanding. "Those lines were cut. When you are given your cue, you speak your lines!" I did as I was instructed, and the rehearsal moved on.

In my efforts to express myself as a Christian, I can recall multiple times when it was my turn to speak . . . and I didn't. I recall sitting around a campfire on a beach as a new acquaintance sprinkled the phrase "Jesus Christ!" into his conversation. How easy it would have been to say, "Do you know Him?" or "Are we having a prayer party here or what?" I think as a young believer I was sometimes embarrassed to express my faith, just as I was sometimes hesitant to share my thoughts on many things.

Sometimes the absurdity of political correctness is a factor in our failure to speak. I sat in a faculty meeting while it was proposed that our school delete references to Christ from our motto. I was trying to think of what I could say that wouldn't be politically offensive when a Hindu faculty member spoke up and said, "What did Christ do that you all find so offensive?" And with that the debate ended, and the issue never surfaced again.

I suppose "speaking the truth in love" is something some of us have to learn. Listen for the line cues, and speak His truth when the opportunity is given.

Ephesians 4:25
"Therefore putting away falsehood, speak truth each one with his neighbor. For we are members of one another."

Prayer
Jesus, guide me in the role you have given me in this life, and prod me to speak for you when I get the cue. Embolden my heart and mind for the spreading of your love. A-men.

Personal Notes:

28

Being You . . . Being Them

DELL HAD A VOICE worthy of any professional opera company and a local reputation for being the guy to call on if you needed a song performed for a special occasion. His short stature made him the perfect actor to play the lead role in *You're a Good Man, Charlie Brown*. He was great in the role. His comic timing and innocent demeanor were perfect. But there was one problem. His voice was too sophisticated. He sang like Pavarotti, not like Charlie Brown. I recall telling him, "Dell, I need Romper Room, and you are giving me the Metropolitan Opera." Fortunately, Dell wasn't a diva. He laughed and teased me about wasting all the money he'd spent on voice lessons and then gave me exactly what we needed in a Charlie Brown singing voice.

Sometimes how we present ourselves as Christians must fit the circumstances for us to make our best witness. That *doesn't* mean going along with the crowd and doing whatever it does regardless of the consequences, but it might mean tempering our witness to gain a hearing.

I belong to a writers group that meets twice a month in a big city. We read new plays aloud for a gathered audience. Over the years I've participated in readings of plays with deeply questionable morals and lots of profane language. Rather than just blatantly object and refuse to take part, I've waited for the discussion/feedback parts of our session to make appropriate comments. Over the years I've built a reputation as the guy who wants to do theater that affirms life and acknowledges God.

I have a play about a Christian missionary in South America who is visited by her father, a theology professor. Besides the great interaction between the two, the play is loaded with the Gospel. When it was read at writers group, the woman who read the missionary part was a bit incredulous that a woman would give her life to serving orphans in a foreign country. I assured her that real people did that kind of thing, and others in the group backed me up. In fact, not once has anyone denigrated the Christian content that underscores everything I write.

In a recent table discussion about antagonists, I started a comment with, "While I'm fully convinced that Jesus is Lord of the universe, . . ." No one batted an eyelash or questioned my world view. I am one of them. I earned my place at the table and can say whatever I want.

1 CORINTHIANS 9:19–23
"For though I was free from all, I brought myself under bondage to all, that I might gain the more. To the Jews I became as a Jew, that I might gain Jews; to those who are under the law, as under the law, that I might gain those who are under the law; to those who are without law, as without law (not being without law toward God, but under law toward Christ), that I might win those who are without law. To the weak I became as weak, that I might gain the weak. I have become all things to all men, that I may by all means save some. Now I do this for the sake of the Good News, that I may be a joint partaker of it."

PRAYER
Jesus, give me the wisdom to know how to be your follower in ways that will please you and attract others. A-men.

PERSONAL NOTES:

29

Love or Law

I DIDN'T KNOW Juan all that well. He approached me after having been an audience member the opening night of our production of *Godspell*. I did know Juan was a relatively conservative Christian, so I bolstered myself for what he might say. I could see something in his countenance, but I wasn't sure if it was anger or something else. He walked right up to me, grabbed both of my shoulders, looked me in the eye, and with a tear in his eye said, "You've done something wonderful for me." Then he gave me a big bear hug and walked away.

In our production of *Godspell* I'd had the prop master make a banner that said "Love" on one side and "Law" on the other. We flopped the banner over, depending on the lines at the time, trying to illustrate what was law and what was love. We crucified Jesus under the law banner. Then, as the notes of "Long Live God" started, I had Jesus come down off the cross. He turned the banner over to the love side, and we added a handful of lines from Matthew 28 so that the last words Jesus spoke were, "He has risen from the dead."

I'm not sure what happened in Juan's life that night. I'm not sure what it was that we did for him, but I suspect his life was touched by grace. I knew the church Juan went to, and while I knew it preached a gospel of grace through faith, I suspect it was the kind of faith you had to demonstrate purposefully and the kind of grace you had to earn. I think maybe our production of *Godspell* and the juxtaposition of law and love set Juan free, at least a little bit. Whatever the case, Juan was in the audience every night for the full run.

The Word Became Flesh

Ephesians 2: 8–9
". . . for *by grace* you have been *saved* through faith, and that not of yourselves; it is the *gift* of God, not of works, that no one would boast." [emphasis added]

Prayer
Jesus, forgive us for thinking we need to earn your love. Help us to yield ourselves to your grace. A-men.

Personal Notes:

30

What Is Acting?

I LOVE SPENDING a couple of class days getting my beginning acting students to really think about what acting is at the most bottom-line, fundamental levels. We do that by way of discussion and me asking lots and lots and lots of questions. Acting looks easy, and there is a reason for that, which I'll explore later, but what do actors really do . . . bottom-line?

I'll save you all the places our discussions go and cut to the chase. Think about this: Actors add the nonverbal communication to the text. Granted, there is a bit more to it than that, especially if we are talking about really good acting, but the bottom line is that actors add nonverbal to the text. The lines of the play are carved in concrete. Anyone can read them and get a sense of the play, but for the play to live, the nonverbal has to be added back in. Any communications specialist will tell you that up to 95% percent of our intended meaning is in the nonverbal part of the communication. Actors learn to put that back into the written text. How actors' voices sound, how their faces look, what they are doing with posture and gestures—all this has a massive influence on the meaning we derive from what they say to us. Actors take the script, which is without all that nonverbal meaning, and add in that meaning.

What does all this have to do with being a Christian? It's the old saying, "Actions speak louder than words." I recall a Christian student relating the story of driving back to campus in a borrowed car and how she was out of money and out of gas, but "Praise Jesus, we made it back to campus." But her non-Christian roommate then had to deal with a car in the parking lot that had no gas in it.

John tells us, "The Word became flesh . . ." That's what we do when we act. We put flesh on words. That's also what we do when we make our Christian witness. That's what Jesus did when He came to show us God's love and grace. He put flesh on the words.

JOHN 1:14
"The Word became flesh, and lived among us. We saw his glory, such glory as of the one and only Son of the Father, full of grace and truth."

PRAYER
Jesus, challenge me when I fail to be your living word. Empower me to be a living witness of your love and grace. A-men.

PERSONAL NOTES:

31

Learning to Hide the Truth in Our Hearts

CAL WAS A PROFESSIONAL ACTOR with many stage, television, and film credits. He'd come to Christ later in life, and through a major serendipity (God thing?) we'd managed to get him to come direct a show for us. My students learned a lot from Cal. I did, too.

I recall one thing he told my students about learning lines. His advice was to start with the very last line your character says. Say the line ten times. Then, go to the line before it and say it ten times. Then, say the very last line again ten times. Then, the line before it ten times, and so on.

I'd never heard this approach to line learning before. I didn't experiment with it since I had no lines to learn, but the cast seemed to think it worked well.

As an acting student, I'd never been advised on how best to learn lines, so I did what most neophyte actors do—I studied the script. I'd run an index card down the pages of my script so that when I got to my cue line, my line was covered. I'd silently read my cue and then try to speak my line from memory, usually having to read it a few times at the very least. The thing is, when on stage, one doesn't read one's cue lines—one hears them. The actor doesn't read his lines off a page—he speaks them from his mind.

Once, when I had a lengthier role, I got a colleague to "play" opposite me, and we read all my scenes onto a cassette tape. Then as I drove my car, went to sleep, went about my day, I listened to those lines over and over and over. To my delight I discovered that in so doing . . . I'd memorized them.

I once stage-managed a production of *Damien*, the one-man show about the priest who ministered to the leper colony in Hawaii. The show runs almost two hours. The actor I was working with recorded the show and then listened to it over and over and over. It worked. He learned the lines in what I'd call record time.

What if we went after God's Word by listening to it over and over and over? What if we committed God's Word to our hearts and minds the same way we go after learning a script? How much would that change our lives? How much would that make us more like Christ?

HEBREWS 4:12
"For the word of God is living and active, and sharper than any two-edged sword, piercing even to the dividing of soul and spirit, of both joints and marrow, and is able to discern the thoughts and intentions of the heart."

PRAYER
Help us all to make a better effort at hiding your Word in our hearts. Especially me. A-men.

PERSONAL NOTES:

32

A Mind in Neutral

"And now, imagine that your brain is a muscle. Squeeze that muscle and get out all the troubles and tensions and distractions that you carry around in your brain." These words spoken by Dr. Sol were a new idea to me. I'd been exposed to various ways to relax my body, but not my mind.

Part of being a performer is being able to shake off the tensions of the world and come into the performance arena without the cares and distractions of our real lives hindering what we do on stage.

As noted before, I stage-managed a production of *Damien*. By request of the actor, I'd turn on some dim stage lighting and play old Gregorian chants over the sound system about a half hour before the house opened. As I went about my business in the booth, I could look out and see Brad on the stage doing relaxation exercises. Brad, who had a high-pressure day job, was trying to leave all of that stress behind. When it was just about curtain time, I'd go to cue him and find him listening to rock music over headphones. Even dancing sometimes. After losing the tensions of the day, he was energizing himself to perform.

When I teach relaxation, I still use Dr. Sol's idea for relaxing the mind, but I go one step further. I ask my students, "Now that your mind is empty, where is it going to go?" I talk about the idea of where one's mind goes when it's in neutral and the act of meditation. I talk about meditating on Scripture or the person of Jesus.

Once, at this point, with a bunch of my acting students lying on the floor, I had a young lady start to quietly weep. Later in private conversation I debriefed that moment with her. I had suggested some verses from Psalm 23 as meditation matter. The phrase "He restores my soul" had hit her like a ton of bricks. Apparently, she'd had a bad family life, and she realized just how much her soul needed restoring. Jesus is clearly the man for that job.

The more we expose our minds to Jesus, the more we will naturally think about Him.

PSALM 23:1–3
"Yahweh is my shepherd: I shall lack nothing. He makes me lie down in green pastures. He leads me beside still waters. He restores my soul. He guides me in the paths of righteousness for his name's sake."

PRAYER
Jesus, please help me to be in touch with the state of my soul. Help me to yield myself to you for restoration. A-men.

PERSONAL NOTES:

33

Adlibbing Truth

I REALLY ENJOY ACTING but don't get to do all that much. One summer we needed to fill a short part in a melodrama, and I just took the role myself. I was on stage with another creative actor, and this play begged for extra silliness. On opening night, I adlibbed a line about a prop, and it got a huge laugh. That was all it took. Jake and I spent the next few moments adlibbing things and getting a couple more good laughs in the process. That scene grew and grew and grew until its original 30 seconds were running a couple of minutes. I was the director, so there was no one to stop us, and no one complained. Jake and I had a good time. Apparently so did the audience. It was a risk, but the silliness of the play allowed for it.

More than once in my Christian walk I've had the urge to adlib. Not long ago I'd driven by a man engaged in some outside work. I'd had some serious conflicts with this person. The Holy Spirit prodded me, and I resisted, but of course the Holy Spirit didn't let up. I drove back and called out, offering assistance. That action opened the door to civil communication, and while we haven't become fast friends, the tension has eased up a great deal.

Another time, I was just starting class when a colleague followed by a handful of students entered my classroom. Turns out he and I'd been scheduled for the same classroom at the same time. Once we'd figured out the error he proclaimed, "Oh, Jesus Christ!" and stormed away with his students. I turned to my class and said, "You all heard it, right here. Dr. Strang was praying in the classroom." I got a big laugh from my class and moved on. But it did call attention to the casual use of Christ's name as an expletive and how that goes against the political correctness standards most academics like to uphold.

This is how Jesus makes us more like Himself. Sometimes it's an adlib.

EPHESIANS 4:15
". . . but speaking truth in love, we may grow up in all things into him, who is the head, Christ."

PRAYER
Jesus, when you prod me to be your person . . . don't let me ignore it. A-men.

PERSONAL NOTES:

34

I Am His

IT WAS A FEELING I hadn't had for a *long* time. I was looking forward to going to rehearsal. For most of my theatrical life I'd always enjoyed the rehearsal process, and I *never ever* dreaded going to rehearsal. Yet, really, seriously, famously, joyously looking forward to rehearsal wasn't always the case. It usually was something like, "Yeah, I'm tired, but I have rehearsal, and I know I'll be energized by the process, so it will all be okay." And it *was* okay. I was like a rehearsal junkie. Regardless of how I felt at the start of a rehearsal, I was always flying high by the end.

But this was different. I hadn't looked forward to rehearsal with this much enthusiasm for a long time, and at first, I couldn't figure out what was different. I'm sure that part of it was being retired. Without a long day of classes and meetings behind me, I simply had more energy and less stress when rehearsal time came. But it was more than that.

Finally, I figured out that I was more excited because . . . these were mine. I wrote these plays. All of them had been workshopped and produced elsewhere, and one was even an award winner, but this was the first time I was directing them. The actors were doing a great job, and it was so much fun watching them put life to the words I'd put on the page. It was seriously fulfilling.

Part of me wonders if my experience isn't a foggy, vague glimpse into God's love for us. We are His. We live out the breath and grace He pours into us. I suspect we make God cry, but I also suspect we make God laugh and sing and shout for joy. We are His, and when we get it right, when we share grace, when we forgive, when we celebrate life . . . I think God is exceedingly glad.

1 JOHN 3:1–2
"See how great a love the Father has given to us, that we should be called children of God! For this cause the world doesn't know us, because it didn't know him. Beloved, now we are children of God, and it is not yet revealed what we will be. But we know that, when he is revealed, we will be like him; for we will see him just as he is."

PRAYER
Lord, may I know in every moment of every day that I am yours. Guide my ways that I might cause you joy. A-men.

PERSONAL NOTES:

35

Why Don't You Tell Them about That!

A COMMUNITY THEATER I helped found billed itself as a family theater. We sought to involve all age groups, and partly to that end some of our board members started a geriatric theater. (That's what they called it, not my choice.) On opening night of the first show, about halfway through act I, with no less than five actors on the stage, the dialogue went off course . . .

A: Um . . . well . . . why don't you tell them about that?
B: No, I think it would be better if "C" told them about that.
C: Actually, it would be better if "D" told them. . . . etc.

Finally, it dawned on me that all five actors had gone up on their lines at the same time. I really don't remember how they worked their way out of it, but the show went on. Amazingly, they got a standing ovation at the end. The show wasn't really all that good, but the audience loved it. In fact, the audience, which was made up of the families and friends of the cast and crew, really, really wanted the show to be good, and so it was.

I suspect that is how Jesus loves us. We forget our lines, miss entrances, turn in a poor performance, and He still says to us, "Come on! You can do this." (That's in the Bible, right?) Jesus isn't waiting for us to fail so that He can scold us. He wants us to succeed in being His people, so He cheers us on. Yeah, we fail. But we have to keep trying in the name of Him who loves us most.

The Word Became Flesh

ISAIAH 49:16
"Behold, I have engraved *you* on the palms of my hands." [emphasis added]

PRAYER
Lord, I can never be grateful enough that you love me and want me to do well. You cheerlead my life, and I couldn't ask for more. A-men.

PERSONAL NOTES:

36

How Did I Do That?

ONE OF MY FAVORITE ACTING STORIES involves the great Laurence Olivier. I've read about this incident in more than one book, so I'm guessing it's as true as can be.

On the night in question, Sir Laurence was absolutely rocking the title role in *King Lear*. It was by all accounts a truly amazing performance. The applause at his curtain call went on and on and on. The cast and crew lined the hallway and applauded him as he went back to his dressing room. But as he walked between them, their applause lessened a bit. Something was wrong. The scowl on his face plowed through their enthusiastic admiration, pushing it aside.

Of course, it fell to the stage manager to see what was amiss. The young man timidly knocked on the dressing room door. It was slammed open by the brooding Olivier.

"What is it?" Sir Laurence demanded, pushing back the stage manager with his pensive countenance alone.

"Sir, you were wonderful this evening!" the stage manager blurted out, "Absolutely amazing! An astonishing performance! Truly remarkable."

Olivier stopped his pacing and became reflective. "Yes, I was good, wasn't I? Very good."

"Oh, yes, sir. You were so very good, sir." The stage manager was still confused but didn't know how to go on.

Olivier glared at the stage manager and demanded "And so?"

Plucking up his courage, the stage manager explained, "Coming down the hall, just now sir, you looked . . . upset. Is something wrong, sir?"

Olivier wilted and finally sat down. "Tonight I was amazing!"

"Yes, sir. You were."

There was a moment of silence before Olivier spoke again. "But I don't know how I did it, and I don't know if I can do it again."

I share this tale with my acting students to underline the need for some kind of intentional approach to acting. No, *there is no one definitive way to approach acting*, and anyone who tries to tell you differently is simply wrong. And for the individual actor, what works for one part may not work for the next, so her approach will always be in a state of flux. Nonetheless, an actor has to have means whereby he begins to approach a role.

I think our walk with Christ is like that. There is no formula we can apply to our lives to get us to the place where God can use us to do His will and do it well. But we have to at least try. We pray and study God's word and worship with the church, and each individual Christian is going to have a unique take on how that is done and its effect in her life. And in the final analysis, when God uses us to do some amazing thing, we have to say, "I don't know how I did that, and I'm not sure I can do it again!" Then we have to add, "I know it's all by God's grace, and I'm just *trying* to be a useable vessel."

PHILIPPIANS 2:13
"For it is God who works in you both to will and to work, for his good pleasure."

PRAYER
Jesus, help me to understand this paradox. Nothing I can do will make me the perfect vessel for your work through me . . . but I must nonetheless try. Help me to yield my will to you. A-men.

PERSONAL NOTES:

37

Who Wrote This?

RANDAL ASKED ME A QUESTION about his character's motivation. His was an appropriate query for an actor to pose to his director. I had to think for a bit. Then I asked Randal some questions, and he and I analyzed the moment more fully. Randal was a touch mystified, and I understood his confusion when he said, "What did you have in mind when you wrote it?"

It wasn't the first time I'd directed my own script, nor was it the first time that I wasn't sure about the motivation of one of my characters. More than once as I've directed an original script from my own pen I've said, "Who wrote this?" The query comes when the lines aren't working and need to be "fixed." This occurs even in scripts for which I've had multiple workshop readings.

Randal's query made me think more deeply about this whole paradox. How can a playwright not know his characters' motivations? How is that possible? I realized quickly that this conundrum exists because I write instinctively. I don't have all the tenets of play analysis in mind when I create a script. What I have in mind is, "I want to tell an amazing story with amazing characters and amazing action." I know a handful of playwrights, and I don't think any of us writes plays via the dictates of script analysis.

Analysis—whether it is of a script or a poem or a novel—is an after-the-fact intellectual/academic pursuit. Writing plays or novels or poems is an affair of the heart and the soul, not the classroom.

Now, don't get me wrong. Script analysis is a valuable tool for both the writer and the director. Analysis has helped me to understand plays I wrote instinctively so that I can make them stronger.

When I sit in the director's chair, I'm also working instinctively, but helping actors figure things out requires at least some bits and pieces of an analytical approach. If I'm going to help the actor, I need to understand that blueprint we call a script.

I think our walk with Christ is at its best when we instinctively act like Him. Asking ourselves, "What would Jesus do?" is analysis. And sometimes analysis is needed. But how much better is it if we naturally, without thinking about it, do and say the things Jesus would do and say.

1 JOHN 2:6
". . . he who says he remains in him ought himself also to walk just like he walked."

PRAYER
Jesus, please grow me to the point that I *am* a Christian, not just trying to act like one. A-men.

PERSONAL NOTES:

38

Unbalanced

THE FIRE ALARM WENT OFF in the middle of acting class. Dr. Sol suggested it would be best if we left the building, so we did. Not too long after the "all clear" was called, Dr. Sol ended class and sent us on our way. As I entered the building, our technical director came running down the hall toward me . . . carrying an unconscious girl. He thrust the limp body into my arms and said, "Meet me in the lobby!" I was confused but obedient. As I reached the lobby, I was surprised to see the technical director's car up on the patio outside the main lobby doors. He grabbed the girl from me, thrust her into the front seat, and was gone. Only then did I realize that the girl's hands looked like shredded flesh.

Long story short, a staff member, who had no business changing main drapes, had taken it upon himself to do so. He'd had students fly in a dead-hung, full-stage drape and take it off the batten . . . violating the first rule of using a counterbalanced fly system. He'd made the system unbalanced, with the heavy end at the top. He hadn't sent anyone up to the fly gallery to take off the counterweights. He'd told the girl to fly the batten out. She'd unlocked the rope at the pin rail, and the now unbalanced counterweight came flying down. She had grabbed the rope to stop it. She was a small person, and the counterweights were heavier than her. The rope sped through her hands, taking flesh with it. The batten moved upward so fast that it flew past the end of its run and traveled upward into the fire-safety sprinkler system, setting off the sprinklers and the alarm in the process, drenching the stage and all the other curtains.

Balance in life can be a tricky thing. The things that happen when we become unbalanced can be disastrous. Being too busy can be a way of being unbalanced.

A student I was mentoring brought me his time management plan. After a quick look I asked, "Why are you planning to have a failure of a semester?" He didn't understand until I pointed out that he'd only left himself 32 hours a week to eat, sleep, and recreate.

Because of our dedication to the art, we theater people can be too busy. Instead of having a life, theater becomes our life. Our life becomes unbalanced, often with disastrous results.

It is far better to manage our lives to prevent the unbalance.

Mark 6:31

"He said to them, 'You come apart into a deserted place, and rest awhile.' For there were many coming and going, and they had no leisure so much as to eat."

Prayer

Jesus, please be the alarm that goes off in my heart when my life becomes unbalanced. Help me to honor what you have done for me by keeping myself healthy in all ways. A-men.

Personal Notes:

39

A Group Effort

WHEN I SIGNED UP for Professor Bartlet's theater graphics class, I didn't think there was all that much to learn about color. I was so astoundingly wrong. Professor Bartlet knew so much about color that he could lecture about it for hours. The test on the color unit was, he said, "simple." He had a deck of a couple hundred cards that showed every shade and variation of every color imaginable. For the exam, he selected a card from the deck, placed it on our desk, and we had to match the color using our own paints. Easy, right? For some, yes, but not for me. I labored for the hour and then stayed in the graphics lab to work on it longer. I don't recall how many times I started over. Soon I had three or four other classmates helping me. They were quite literally helping me take a test. We finally found the match. I paper-clipped my color card to my paper and scrawled a note on it before dropping it in Professor Bartlet's mailbox. In the note, I told the truth: "Prof. Bartlet, to find this color, no less than four other people helped me. It was a group effort and is not the result of just my own work."

To my surprise, I got an "A" on the exam. Professor Bartlet was a bit of an upper-class snob, far better than his students, but to my surprise he included a reply note. "Richard: Thank you for your honesty. But after all isn't that what theater is all about, the group effort?"

In the past year, I've become aware of four ministries that suffered because the leaders had a hard time dealing with the successes of their subordinates. In one instance, a youth pastor's program was shut down, even though it was obviously the most successful program in the whole church. The jealous lead pastor said he was trying to save the youth pastor from burnout.

As Christians and as theater artists, our success is *our* success. It's one of the things I love most about being a theater artist and about being a Christian. *We* have to do this together to make it work. God expects *us* to do so.

1 Corinthians 12:12
"For as the body is one, and has many members, and all the members of the body, being many, are one body; so also is Christ."

Prayer
Lord, thank you for making me a part of "we." A-men.

Personal Notes:

40

His Approval

IT IS A RARE and intimidating privilege to get to direct a play and then have the playwright come to a performance. I was directing Jeff Barker's *Unspoken for Time*. I'd managed to get a grant to bring Jeff to campus to see the show and talk to my students about playwriting. We sat next to each other on opening night. About halfway through act II there is a critical moment when the lead character goes through an inner crisis, has a moment of inner clarity, and then makes a life-changing decision. We'd worked the blocking and business of that moment many times in rehearsal. That night the actress did a good job, and you could hear a pin drop in the silence of the full house. Then I felt a poke in my shoulder. I looked over at Jeff to see him giving me the thumbs up sign. Wow, wow, wow! What an affirmation! How wonderful to have this playwright, who I deeply respected, enjoy my direction of his work.

I've noted before that as a Christian I do my best and then wallow in an ocean of grace. I know I can't earn His grace. It's a gift. And yet I hope the day will come when my Master says to me, "Well done, my good and faithful servant." Wow, wow, wow!

2 CORINTHIANS 10:18
"For it isn't he who commends himself who is approved, but whom the Lord commends."

The Word Became Flesh

Prayer

Master, I covet your love and approval. Help me to do my best. Thank you that I get to revel in your grace! A-men.

Personal Notes:

41

That's How He Wrote It

In Jeff Barker's *Unspoken for Time* there is a series of monologues from women telling their stories of abuse. As it is written in the script, each woman tells her story sitting on a chair that gets added to a circle at the end of her story. Then all the women are together on their chairs at the finale.

When I directed the show, I had each woman place her stool down center for her monologue and then move it to a platform that was 18 inches lower than the stage. That way, the audience was always looking past those chairs to the action of the play. The chairs were a visual reminder of the damaged lives. At intermission on opening night, Jeff told me how he liked the circle of chairs that was growing on the lift in front of the stage. I had to tell him, "That's how you wrote it." He, of course, knew that was how he'd written it, but like any playwright, he enjoyed seeing his words come to life on stage in ways that clearly worked in the way he'd intended. He knew what should happen and was glad to see it in action.

God knows our frame. God knows how He intended us to live. God knows what He intended for us to do and be. God wrote the script for our lives. And while it is not how we earn our way into His grace and love, if we want the most fulfilling lives, if we want to make God smile, we do well to follow His script.

Proverbs 16:9
"A man's heart plans his course, but Yahweh directs his steps."

The Word Became Flesh

PROVERBS 19:21
"There are many plans in a man's heart, but Yahweh's counsel will prevail."

PRAYER
God of my life, guide me in all wisdom and love so that my steps will be your steps. A-men.

PERSONAL NOTES:

42

I Had All the Fun

MRS. CALLAHAN and I were taking a bunch of our students to a vocal workshop in the nearby big town. As we drove, we talked about our small community, the small college there, the nice theater at that small college, and how the building was underused, especially in the summers. Those conversations continued into the school year, and the following fall we gathered up the local people who we thought would be willing to serve on the board of a community theater.

Fast-forward to the following June when we opened *You're a Good Man, Charlie Brown* as the first Summer Repertory Theater at Blackburn College production. Amazingly, as the kids marched down the aisle toward the stage in the opening number, we got a standing ovation. Yes, that's right, a standing ovation at the top of the show.

Fast-forward again 13 years later when I was leaving Blackburn. The cast and crew of our summer show gave me the I Had All the Fun Award. See, back when Mrs. Callahan and I were trying to get the whole thing started, I had suggested to her that she be the executive director and I be the artistic director. When she asked me what that meant, I said, "It means you do all the work, and I have all the fun." A couple years later I reminded her of that conversation, and she said, "You were right." (Although we both admittedly were doing lots of work and having lots of fun.)

I wouldn't be a theater artist if it wasn't loads of fun. What about my Christian walk? There have been times in my life, thankfully short periods, when the conservative church had me convinced that Christians aren't supposed to have fun, and especially that being a Christian isn't supposed to be fun. I think nothing could be further from the truth. I recall a speaker, Donna Dong, at the Reconcilers Conference, talking about our presence in God's Kingdom as one big party, a party where there is room at the table for everyone. Recently, via social media, I told someone, "I'm not so sure that being a Christian, for me, is so much about heaven and hell as it is about getting to know the Lord of the universe and partying with Him forever." I guess that sounds a touch flippant and heretical, but only if you think being a Christian *isn't* supposed to be fun.

1 Peter 1:8–9
". . . whom not having known you love; in whom, though now you don't see him, yet believing, you rejoice greatly with joy unspeakable and full of glory—receiving the result of your faith, the salvation of your souls."

Romans 15:13
"Now may the God of hope fill you with all joy and peace in believing, that you may abound in hope, in the power of the Holy Spirit."

Prayer
Lord, I know there will be tribulation in this world, but never let me forget that that there is fun and joy in knowing you. A-men.

Personal Notes:

43

What Time Does the Show Start . . . Really?

I WAS MYSTIFIED when I saw the poster. Show time was 7:30 p.m. I thought that information was clear to everyone, but the poster said 7:00 p.m. I wondered what was going on. I'd been hired by a community theater board to direct for them, and they were handling box office and advertising (as they should). Finally, I got hold of the board member who was responsible for the advertising.

"All along you've told me that show time was 7:30, but the poster says 7:00. Have things changed, or is this a mistake, or what?"

I could hardly believe her reply.

"All kinds of people show up late, so I thought I'd advertise the show as starting at 7:00 so they'd all be here by 7:30."

Really? Seriously?

For every performance of our two-weekend run people showed up well before 7:00 and were dismayed at the lengthy wait. The deception only hurt the reputation of our theater. The theater had lied to people, hoping to get the desired behavior from them, only to the detriment of all involved.

I've been through a lot of evangelism training. With my years has come at least a taste of wisdom, and as I reflect on that training, I know some of it wasn't good. I recall one speaker telling us that we should "show the bait, but not the hook," meaning that we can't reveal what's really behind our attempts to win people to Christ. I also recall training about "friendship evangelism." Seriously? Become someone's "friend" to win the person to Christ? I don't think that kind of ulterior motive fits any real definition of "friend." If we can't be honest with friends and acquaintances about our Christianity, then what can we be honest about?

Philippians 4:8–9
"Finally, brothers, whatever things are true, whatever things are honorable, whatever things are just, whatever things are pure, whatever things are lovely, whatever things are of good report; if there is any virtue, and if there is any praise, think about these things. The things which you learned, received, heard, and saw in me: do these things, and the God of peace will be with you."

Prayer
Lord, only you and I know the real me. I suspect you know me better than I do. Help me be the real me with all people, especially as my selfhood pertains to loving you. A-men.

Personal Notes:

44

Finding God's Kingdom

BRAD WAS A DAIRY FARMER who'd been blessed with a wonderful speaking voice. He was frequently tapped to do some "performance work" in worship services. On the Sunday in question, Brad was doing two monologues about Nehemiah. The first monologue told how Nehemiah received the call to go and rebuild Jerusalem.

As I listened to Brad standing down center, in a thrown-together costume, I thought he did a nice job, although I think he was still wearing his watch. The second monologue was about Nehemiah arriving at Jerusalem and surveying the broken walls and what it felt like to see God's city in ruin. As I watched Brad "perform," I noticed a glint on his cheek! Brad's Nehemiah had a tear running down his face. I looked around the congregation, and Brad wasn't the only one with tears. Suddenly, I was no longer the analytical theater guy appraising Brad's performance. Suddenly, I felt like an Old Testament prophet whose heart was broken because God's city was broken.

Here was a dairy farmer, with no theatrical training whatsoever, breaking our hearts in a moment of amazing theater.

One thing I believe to be true about theater is this, "Good theater is where you find it." I've paid hundreds of dollars to see big name actors perform in top tier shows only to be severely disappointed in the whole thing. I've also paid only a few dollars for an educational or community theater performance that seriously rocked the house. That morning in church, Brad gave us a theatrical moment that touched us at the core of our being, and it didn't cost us a dime.

I think the Kingdom of God is also "where you find it." A sermon at a giant church with a massive worship team may not touch your heart at all, but some words of wisdom spoken by a humble street person could change your life forever.

I recall having a bad day in my walk with Christ, a day full of failures. I confessed my shortcomings to a friend and told her I thought God was showing me my sin. My friend's response was clearly from His Wisdom: "God must love you a lot to deal that specifically with you!"

There was God's Kingdom dumped in my lap, without the accoutrements of a big church or a talented worship team. God's Kingdom is where you find it . . . and sometimes it finds you.

JAMES 4:10
"Humble yourselves in the sight of the Lord, and he will exalt you."

PRAYER
Lord, bless me with the eyes and ears to see and hear your Kingdom whenever I encounter it. A-men.

PERSONAL NOTES:

45

The Most Beautiful Thing I've Seen All Day

I THINK IT WAS AT A FIRST DRESS REHEARSAL for a production of *Oliver!* at our summer theater. Cast and crew gathered in one big circle, I gave the usual pep talk, and we did some vocal and physical warm-ups. Then we held hands all around and made eye contact. As we did so, it occurred to me how amazingly beautiful this was. This was a more beautiful part of God's creation than the Grand Canyon or the starry, starry night. I think some will argue with me here, but the psalmist tells us that human beings are made "a little less than angels." Mankind is more beautifully and wonderfully made than any other physical part of earthly creation. After all, God created this world for His relationship with humanity. That's what it's all about.

I told my cast that they were more beautiful than any artwork made by any human being. That they were more beautiful than any other part of God's creation. That the Taj Mahal, the Grand Canyon, the Mona Lisa, the aurora borealis, while amazing and beautiful, were nothing compared to them. We are God's best artwork. I told them that they were "the most beautiful thing I'd seen all day." It became part of our preshow mantra for that cast and every one after. My "What is this?" was responded to with "The most beautiful thing I've seen all day."

When I first became chair of Bethel College's theater department, the drama club made it the slogan on their shirt that year. "The Most Beautiful Thing I've Seen All Day." And they were. And you are.

The Word Became Flesh

Psalms 8: 4–5
". . . what is mankind that you are mindful of them, human beings that you care for them? You have made them a little lower than the angels and crowned them with glory and honor."

Prayer
Jesus, help me to remember that every human being is a glorious part of your creation. A-men.

Personal Notes:

46

What Lives On?

IT WAS A HIGH SCHOOL PRODUCTION of *Guys and Dolls*, and it was a visual feast. Every bit of every set, every stitch of every costume, every ray of light and puddle of shadow, and every prop, both large and small, was dazzling. I recall that the gambling scene in the sewer made me feel like I could walk onto the stage and go down that sewer tunnel forever. A good fifty years later I can still see it in my mind's eye.

I can also recall what I and the rest of the audience talked about after the show. We talked almost exclusively about the technical aspects, the sets, the lights, the costumes, yet said nothing about the performers. The tech, while brilliant, had literally outshined the cast and crew.

Some many years later, I was directing a production of *The Music Man*. After paying the royalties, we had little money left over for sets, costumes, etc. That, of course, didn't stop us. For the salesman train scene at the beginning, I had actors sit back-to-back on black acting boxes and let their well-choreographed actions sell the existence of the train. We had a piano on a rolling platform for Mrs. Paroo's music studio and a small garden bridge for the footbridge scene. We played most of the rest of the show on an empty stage in front of a down stage curtain. For costumes, I showed the kids some appropriate era pictures and let them find their own. I had to loan a jacket to a young man who simply had nothing. We worked hard on our *performance* and had a good time. We got a standing ovation on both nights of our short run and were done.

A couple days later, sitting in a pizza parlor booth, I overheard two older couples talking about the show. They didn't say one word about the lack of tech. What they were most impressed with was how "confident" the cast had been. They talked about how "real" the performance had seemed. These couples had been impressed with the live people in the show and weren't looking for technical trappings.

How like that is our Christian witness? Our non-Christian friends and acquaintances don't care where we go to church or what version of the Bible we read. They aren't looking at our WWJD bracelets, our cross necklaces, or our fish symbol bumper stickers. What they see is us, not our trappings. Kind of scary, but oh so real.

2 CORINTHIANS 3:2
"You are our letter, written in our hearts, known and read by all men."

PRAYER
Lord, may the script of my life be written by your hand, that I might be a constant witness of your glory and grace to all who interact with me. A-men.

PERSONAL NOTES:

47

What Does It Mean to Be Christian, If Not This?

IT WAS 10:30 AT NIGHT. After giving notes to the cast and reviewing some tech stuff with the stage manager, I was finally on my way home. As I passed by the rehearsal hall the door was still ajar and something was going on in there. I poked my head in and wasn't noticed by the stage manager and the cast members who were in there working. They were helping Amy get caught up on learning her blocking and her lines. Amy had to take a break from rehearsal for medical reasons. She was back now and without any instruction from me, so my stage manager and a handful of cast had stayed late to help her. All of them were students and had full days of classes and rehearsals behind them, with mountains of homework yet ahead of them. But they stayed to help Amy. I witnessed this kind of "service to others" attitude in action with my Bethel students time and time again.

I recall a conversation with Jane late one spring semester:

"Jane," I said, "what are you doing this summer?"

Jane, who was an MK (missionary kid), didn't miss a beat and casually said, "In June I'll be doing translation work for medical missionaries in the Amazon basin."

"Wow. What about July and August?"

"Oh, I'll be at an AIDS hospice in India. That should be interesting!"

Interesting, indeed.

What does it mean to be a Christian theater artist, if not this?

GALATIANS 6:2
"Bear one another's burdens, and so fulfill the law of Christ."

PRAYER
Master, may I be someone who is not afraid to ask for help but also someone who offers help before others ask. A-men.

PERSONAL NOTES:

48

Do the Work and Trust God to Provide

I WAS AT A COLLEGE THEATER FESTIVAL. I knew that Cal was also a participant. He had a long list of TV and film credits, and I knew who he was, but I didn't really expect to meet him or talk to him.

I was sitting, reading through the festival schedule, when I heard someone say, "Bethel! House of God!" I was wearing my Bethel College hat and the voice was none other than Cal's. Turns out that he was a late-in-life conversion and was now an evangelical Catholic. I introduced myself, and we had a short conversation. I didn't think too much more about the encounter.

During the following year it occurred to me that I should explore what it would take to get Cal to come direct a show for us. At that same festival a year later, again wearing my Bethel College hat, I approached Cal, planning to talk to him about what it would take to get him to direct for us. Before I spoke a word he said, "Bethel College! I should come direct a show for you." We talked and made plans.

During the next year there were multiple times when I thought our plans would fall through because the resources were just not available. At one point I had to tell Cal, "I don't have all the financial resources I need to pay your requested salary." Cal's quick response was, "That's okay. Let's just do the work and trust God to provide."

Cal would direct for us in the fall, and he came for a visit late in the spring before. He and I were together when I got a call from my office administrator.

The Word Became Flesh

"Rich, we got a letter from the Whitman Foundation!" The Whitman Foundation was a place we applied to for a grant to help us bring Cal to our campus.

"Open it!" I said. "Read it to us."

"Oh!" she said. "It's a check!" The check was the exact amount we needed to pay the rest of Cal's salary. By the time Cal arrived on campus the following fall, all the things needed for his visit had come together, and they had God's fingerprints all over them.

We had done the work and God provided.

Ephesians 3:20–21
"Now to him who is able to do exceedingly abundantly above all that we ask or think, according to the power that works in us, to him be the glory in the assembly and in Christ Jesus to all generations forever and ever. A-men."

Prayer
Help me to find the work I should do to grow your Kingdom on earth, and help me to trust you to provide. A-men.

Personal Notes:

49

Fear or Respect?

RONALD WAS a world-famous choreographer and director. Today, years after his death, his style is still recognized and used all over the professional musical theater world. Producers loved him for what they would gain from a show he put together, but not so much his cast and crew.

Apparently Ronald was a tyrant. He belittled, berated, cursed, yelled at, humiliated, insulted, and demeaned all those he supervised. He was the god of his world, and if you weren't subservient . . . watch out.

He was so disliked that his cast and crew would make fun of him behind his back. They cared so little for him that once, when they could have warned him of impending danger, they didn't say a thing and he fell off the stage into the orchestra pit.

He was indeed a great theater artist, but a horrible human being at the same time.

There is an old adage that floats around the theater world. It's the idea that if you want to do well in professional theater, don't be hard to work with. It's not always true.

I had a friend who became a writer on a popular TV sitcom. He related to me how the lead performer was an egotistic, uncaring human being. The performer had the crew members wear shirts with numbers on them so she wouldn't have to remember their names. Eventually that show was canceled, and the word on the street was that it was due to the lead performer being hard to work with.

You'd think Christians would be immune to this kind of behavior. Unfortunately, it isn't so. I've been around a handful of churches and ministries where the leader(s) motivated others through fear instead of love. I once realized that I was doing something a certain way so that the artistic director of the organization I worked for wouldn't get angry. That moment motivated me to look elsewhere for employment.

High quality work should be expected at every level of theater, especially in the professional world. My friend who wrote for the sitcom liked to say, "Quality always wins." But there are ways to hold people to the expectation of high quality without demeaning their humanness.

LUKE 6:31
"As you would like people to do to you, do exactly so to them."

PRAYER
Jesus, the world of theater can be a harsh place. Grant me the gift of truth endowed with kindness, that I might grow quality work in your name that honors the humanness of all those around me. A-men.

PERSONAL NOTES:

50

To Be or Not To Be

APART FROM THE CONTEXT, it's a movie or it's a play—how do you know someone is acting? I love asking that question to my first level acting classes. The answer is simple: apart from the circumstances, you *don't* know that someone is acting. When performers are doing a great job of acting, the goal is for them to look like real people doing real things. If they look like actors who are acting, then they have failed.

Apart from context, how do you know someone is being a Christian? What is it about my life or your life that says to the world, "This person is a follower of Jesus"?

It would be a mistake to try to answer that question with a list of things that indicate someone is a Christian. Sure, there are things we could point to that indicate a person *isn't* a Christian; the Ten Commandments is a good place to start. But even so, Christians still sin, fail, blow it, break one or more of the Ten Commandments.

Back in the 1960s I had a friend who joined a group of Christians that by most standards would be considered a cult. He discovered quickly that if he didn't do things in exactly the ways they expected, he couldn't be one of them. Some mainstream Christian churches can act in a similar manner. Fortunately, my friend saw the real light and got out of the cult.

Now, don't go telling people that I said mainstream Christian churches are like cults! Far from it. But even in my own congregation there are expectations for involvement. Yet I know that if my *only* involvement was to come to worship on Sunday, I would still be loved and welcomed. I can gladly say that I get involved in my church in the areas where I have gifts and enjoy using those gifts.

You've probably gathered from these devotions that, for me, staying close to Jesus is a huge part of being a Christian. In my case, that means studying the Gospels, prayer, and worship. Yeah, I know that's a traditional cliché list of things Christians do, but it's what works for me.

And what do I do that people could identify as me being a Christian? I don't have a good handle on that, except to say that I try to stay close to Jesus and live as honestly as I can. The hope is that His love and grace shine through.

1 CORINTHIANS 15:10
"But by the grace of God I am what I am."

PRAYER
Master, I want my heart, my mind, my spirit, my soul to be stayed on you, that I might be your light in this world. Help me to recognize when I am following behaviors to emulate them instead of following you. A-men.

PERSONAL NOTES:

51

Quantity Versus Quality

JAY AND RAY brought me their tentative rehearsal schedule . . . and I was horrified. They were putting together a musical production at our small college, and my division chair and provost agreed to let me supervise their production (instead of directing) as part of my teaching load for a semester. (Blessings on them both.)

Jay and Ray both had vision and energy and some theater experience. However, I was quick to discover that their experience wasn't all of the best kind. Their rehearsal schedule was for four hours a day, seven days a week, for eight weeks, and they expected the whole cast to be there for every rehearsal. Apparently that's what had been modeled for them by their high school directors. In professional theater, yes, everyone is there all the time and you rehearse your brains out. But this was educational theater, and their very large cast all had 12 or more credits of classwork to do, not to mention the other 15 hours of work they had to put in for the institution. (This was at a "work college," where every student engaged in work to keep costs down.) This rehearsal schedule was too much. It would wear out the cast and crew, people would get sick, grades would suffer, and it all would be bad for the theater department's reputation.

They were astounded when I told them, "No!" I told them that they would rehearse three hours a night, for six weeks. That was our standard, and it worked just fine. I also told them they would plan out, in specific detail, what was to be covered at each rehearsal and only call in those people who were needed for that rehearsal. I'm sure Jay and Ray both thought I didn't know what I was doing. They had bought into the idea that lots of rehearsal was how you made quality theater. The truth is that quality rehearsal is how you make quality theater.

I sat them down and we planned out a specific schedule of blocking and working scenes, lines due, etc. And it took a lot more planning work than they were used to. I also dropped in on rehearsal to make sure they were starting and ending on time and using the time wisely. And they put together a great show.

In our Christian walk we can make the mistake of too much rehearsal. We can go to every church activity, every class, every worship service, and every prayer service. While all those things are good, if they become our whole life, then we haven't left the salt-shaker to become part of the stew.[1]

Just like how doing lots of rehearsal in and of itself doesn't make a quality performance, doing lots of "Christian" in and of itself doesn't make us the people Jesus wants us to be.

Matthew 6:7
"In praying, don't use vain repetitions, as the Gentiles do; for they think that they will be heard for their much speaking."

Prayer
Lord, while I understand that following you means being part of the church, help me also to understand that being part of the church isn't the same as following you. A-men.

Personal Notes:

52

To Achieve Quality . . .

ALTHOUGH I WAS SERIOUSLY EXCITED about the possibility of being part of this particular show, I left without auditioning.

The director revealed that the rehearsals would be one night a week, for three hours, for ten weeks. After all, that's how the class was scheduled. When someone questioned this scarcity of work, the director simply said, "Well, we'll all have to do a lot of work on our own."

Really? Produce a major musical, with a script that is nearly 200 pages long, with amateur performers, in only thirty hours of rehearsal? Not possible. The result can only be a disaster. And it was. I talked to some who had gone to see that production, and they felt embarrassed for everyone involved.

I have seen well-performed theater that was put together in a week. But the situation was a small cast musical, performed by professionals, at a summer stock theater that rehearsed all day long, all week long.

I think it is a truth about life that quality anything takes time to achieve. So, too, our spiritual life. I've known a few spiritual giants. They were people who knew the Scripture backwards, forwards, and sideways. They prayed about as much as they breathed. The better I got to know them, the more I realized they had wrapped their heads and hearts around the King of the cosmos. And they certainly would never have considered themselves spiritual giants. Those people didn't become that way overnight. They had made wise decisions about how they would purposefully pursue God in every way possible. They had followed up those decisions with actions: studying the Bible and seeking His face in earnest prayer.

They were also people who seemed to be able to listen for and to God's voice. They knew how to identify God's touch on their lives. All of this took time and effort on their part, and it wasn't always easy.

MATTHEW 6:33
"But seek first God's Kingdom, and his righteousness; and all these things will be given to you as well."

DEUTERONOMY 4:29
"But from there you shall seek Yahweh your God, and you shall find him, when you search after him with all your heart and with all your soul."

PRAYER
Lord God, thank you for making yourself knowable to us. Thank you for revealing yourself through your Word and your creation. Motivate me to do the work, spend the time, make the real effort to know you as fully as possible. A-men.

PERSONAL NOTES:

53

Of Arrogance and Humility

IT WAS THE LAST TIME I spoke to Hank. He was a graduating senior, and this was his exit interview. He proceeded to tell us all the things he was sure he should have learned but didn't. He made it very clear that, as far as he was concerned, we had failed him.

I reminded Hank about the college catalogue and course descriptions. Had he not looked at those before he applied? I reminded Hank about our course evaluation process. I asked him, "How is it that at the end of your last semester here you finally realized we aren't teaching you what you want to learn?"

I'd been around enough theater students to have observed this phenomenon before. As a student, I too had been guilty of it. There were times I was sure that I knew better than my professors what this theater thing was really all about.

Then there was Ann. I'd seen her in a high school musical production. I gave her my card and invited her to attend my institution. To my delight, she did. She came to my class already a fine actor. Finding scene work that challenged her was no small task. It was a treat to have her in class.

She left us because our institution was just too costly. She'd visit once in a while and drop by to say "Hi." Once she poked her head into my office and said, "I learned so much from you!" Ann didn't know it, but I was in a bad mood at the time from, once again, having to convince the school's administration that, "Yes, we do need a full-time costumer!" Her compliment made my day.

Ann had come to campus prepared to learn. Hank had come to demonstrate that he'd already "arrived" as an artist.

We aren't immune from this kind of arrogance in terms of our spiritual walk. I know there have been times in my life, especially in my youth, when my inner dialogue went something like this . . . "If that person would only commit fully to the Lord, then their troubles would dissolve." How astoundingly arrogant of me! How completely inaccurate. As theater artists and as Christians, we never ever "arrive" but are in a constant state of learning and growth.

I recall sitting at table with a man who has a PhD in theater, is a published author of books about theater and ministry, and is head of the theater program at an internationally known church. I told him, "Fred, you are the consummate Christian theater artist and yet you are a model of humility for all of us." His point-proving answer was, "Oh, I don't know about that."

JAMES 4:6
"But he gives more grace. Therefore it says, 'God resists the proud, but gives grace to the humble.'"

PROVERBS 29:23
"A man's pride brings him low, but one of lowly spirit gains honor."

PRAYER
Jesus, smite my arrogance, cultivate my humility. A-men.

PERSONAL NOTES:

54

Don't Do It!

"Don't pursue theater as a profession unless there is absolutely nothing else you'd like to do for the rest of your life."

I've heard this statement from almost every theater teacher I've ever had, and I told my own students the same. Theater is a tough row to hoe. First, you have to have some talent. On top of that, you need good training. Beyond that, you need a break or a connection or some kind of back door into the world of professional theater. Most of all, you have to be tenacious. You have to go after it. You can't wait for theater to come to you because it won't.

Ellie had dreams of becoming a professional make-up artist. When I saw her six months after graduation, I asked how grad school was going . . . It wasn't. After all her talk and dreams, she hadn't applied to any graduate program anywhere. To state the obvious, one gets a career in professional make-up by going after it.

Sandra is a working actress. We've stayed in touch via social media, and I enjoy watching her career, which she has worked and worked and worked to make happen. Sandra has gone to audition after audition and worked all kinds of jobs in between acting gigs to pay the bills. Even as a student, Sandra wanted to learn everything about all aspects of theater. Even though her goal was acting, when she left us she was capable of doing just about anything a production needed.

I remember sitting in my office angry and frustrated and at my wit's end about . . . just about everything going on in my department.

I pushed away from my desk and realized chapel was just about to start. I needed to escape, and chapel was as good a place as any. When I got there it occurred to me that I hadn't been to chapel or church for over three weeks. I couldn't think of the last time I'd intentionally taken some time out to pray. I wasn't even sure where my Bible was.

I'm the *last* person in the world to suggest that God's love for me or His presence in my life depends on what I do. But *my* interaction with that love, *my* enjoyment of that presence, *my* celebration of Him and His creation do depend on what I do. I recently told a friend that I wasn't so sure that being a Christian was so much about heaven or hell as it was about being with Jesus and getting to celebrate who He is forever.

If you want a life in theater, you have to go after it every day. If you want to walk with Jesus, you have to put on your walking shoes and follow after Him every day.

MATTHEW 13:44–46
"Again, the Kingdom of Heaven is like a treasure hidden in the field, which a man found, and hid. In his joy, he goes and sells all that he has, and buys that field. Again, the Kingdom of Heaven is like a man who is a merchant seeking fine pearls, who having found one pearl of great price, he went and sold all that he had, and bought it."

PRAYER
Help me to be diligent in pursuing you every moment. A-men.

PERSONAL NOTES:

Endnotes

Devotional 25

[1] Os Guinness, *God in the Dark: The Assurance of Faith Beyond a Shadow of Doubt* (Wheaton, IL: Crossway Books, 1996).

Devotional 26

[1] Peter Brook, *The Empty Space: A Book About the Theatre: Deadly, Holy, Rough, Immediate* (New York: Scribner, 1995).

Devotional 51

[1] Rebecca Manley Pippert, *Out of the Salt Shaker and into the World* (Downer's Grove, IL: InterVarsity Press, 1999).

Scripture Index

Old Testament
Deuteronomy
4:29   104
Psalms
8:4   90
23   64
23:1–3   64
37:4   3, 4
119:11   2
141:2   40
Proverbs
   23
3:3   2
3:5–6   8
12:15   12
12:18   10
16:9   81
16:24   42
19:21   82
29:23   106
Isaiah
41:10   8
49:16   70

New Testament
Matthew
6:7   102
6:21   6
6:33   104
13:44–46   108
14:29   26
Mark
5:35   36
6:31   76

Luke
6:31   98
John
1:14   52, 60
14:4–5   18
14:10   16
14:26   38
Romans
8:28   32
15:13   84
1 Corinthians
9:19–23   56
12:7   38
12:12   78
15:10   100
2 Corinthians
3:2   92
10:18   79
Galatians
1:10   46
6:2   94
Ephesians
2:8–9   58
3:20–21   96
4:15   66
4:15–16   34
4:25   54
4:29   24, 30, 44
4:30   14
Philippians
1:6   48
2:3   28
2:13   72

Scripture Index

4:8–9   86

Colossians
   4:6   42
   4:29   32

1 Thessalonians
   5:12–13   28

2 Timothy
   1:7   26

Hebrews
   4:12   62
   10:24   42

James
   4:6   106
   4:8   22
   4:10   88
   5:13   40

1 Peter
   1:8–9   84
   2:15   36
   5:6–11   50
   5:8   20

1 John
   2:6   74
   3:1–2   68

Revelation
   14:7   40

Subject Matter Index

abiding, in Jesus, 18
acting, 59, 72, 99
acting class, fire alarm during, 75
acting teacher, bringing students to tears, 44
actions, speaking louder than words, 59
actors
    adding nonverbal communication, 59
    asking about motivation, 73
    with cancer, 37
    drawing a complete blank, 15
    five losing their lines at the same time, 69
    Godless years in TV, 37
    as more animated than cardboard pieces, 51
actress, becoming a working, 107
adlibbing, truth, 65–66
affirmation, to the director by the playwright, 79
AIDS hospice in India, MK (missionary kid) working at, 93
all things, becoming to all men, 56
analysis, as an intellectual/academic pursuit, 73
ancient Hebrews, wore God's Word on their heads, 2
angry yelling, having no place in rehearsal, 9
approach, to acting as always in a state of flux, 72
approval, of those whom the Lord commends, 79

arm, writing on, 1
arrogance, 106
artistic vision, as a big-time risk, 26
audience, 13, 69

balance, in life as a tricky thing, 76
Barker, Jeff, playwright, 79
basics, ignoring, 40
being too busy, as unbalanced, 76
Bible
    people called on by God to take big risks, 26
    people finding God's call as major life changes, 4
body of Christ, 34, 78
bosses, 27, 28
Bottom (character), not sounding like a donkey, 11
brain, engaging before opening one's mouth, 23
brokenness, of the world, 45
Brook, Peter, director, 51
burdens, bearing one another's, 94

call of the Lord, discerning, 26
calling on my life, of God, 32
Camelot, famous vocalist appearing in, 27
cast, directory becoming one with, 51
Cats, as a risk, 26
chairs, as a visual reminder of damaged lives, 81
character, needing motivation, 41
characterization, changes in, 29
children of God, 68

115

Subject Matter Index

choreographer and director, acting as a tyrant, 97
Christ. *See* Jesus Christ
Christian content, of the author's writing, 56
Christian walk. *See* walk with Christ
Christianity, being honest about, 86
Christians
  as being fun, 84
  being sure about being, 50
  being with Jesus, 108
  fitting the circumstances, 55
  knowing if someone is being, 99
  knowing the place of theater arts, 51
  never ever "arriving," 106
  still sinning, 99
classroom, praying in, 65–66
color, matching in our own paints, 77
communication glitch, solving with proximity, 21
community theaters, director responsible for everything, 33
complications, accepting in life, 18
concentration trick, of raising one foot up, 19–20
confidence, based on context, 45
context, as everything, 45–46
course evaluation process, reminding an arrogant student about, 105
creative work, directing as, 49
cues, missing, 19
cult, group of Christians as, 99

dairy farmer, amazing theater performance by, 87
Damien, stage-managing a production of, 62, 63
deception, hurting the reputation of the theater, 85
desires of your heart, delighting in, 4
devil, walking around like a roaring lion, 50
directing, as creative work, 49

director
  becoming one with the cast, 51
  with cancer, 37
  famous coming to direct a show, 95
  feedback from, 11
  making script changes, 29
  responsible for everything in a small community theater, 33
  script analysis as a tool for, 73–74
  solving a problem calmly, 43–44
  as a tyrant, 97
distance, from God because we have moved, 21
Dong, Donna, on God's Kingdom as one big party, 84
donkey, 9, 11–12
drawing a complete blank, as an actor, 15

Easter pageant, playing a Pharisee in, 13
encouragement, as a spiritual gift, 42
evangelism training, 85
exit interviews, from graduating seniors, 105
expectations, in mainstream Christian churches, 99–100

failure, 9, 26
faith, 15, 53
families, involved in a production, 9
family, feeling from working on a production, 33–34
family theater, community theater as, 69
favor, seeking of men or of God, 46
fear, 26, 44
feedback, receiving, 11
fire alarm, in the middle of acting class, 75
flesh, putting on, 52, 60
fly system, using a counterbalanced, 75
follower, asking for wisdom to know how to be, 56

Subject Matter Index

fool, as right in his own eyes, 12
foot off the floor, raising for concentration, 19–20
"friendship evangelism," 85–86

God
  calling people to things, 4
  crying out to, 17
  drawing near to, 22
  emotions for us, 67–68
  as the focus of my soul, 6
  grace of, 100
  handling the tough stuff, 50
  hanging out with, 46
  Kingdom of, 87–88, 104, 108
  knowing how He intended us to live, 81
  pursuing in every way possible, 103–4
  relationship with humanity, 89
  serving to find direction, 28
  sin hurting, 13–14
  trusting to provide, 95
  working in us to will and to work, 72
Godless years, as a TV actor, 37
God's Word. *See* Word, of God
Godspell, banner with "Love" and "Law," 57
good signs, moments of confusion, uncertainty, and doubt as, 49
good theater, as where you find it, 87
grace
  extending, 8
  as a gift with hope, 79
  giving to the humble, 106
  of God, 72
  of Jesus, 48
  yielding ourselves to, 58
gratitude, for God's love, 70
group effort, 77–78
Guys and Dolls, high school production of, 91

hard questions, finding answers to, 50
healing, bringing to colleagues, 44
heart
  God giving you desires of, 4
  hiding truth in, 61–62
  of a man, 81, 82
helpfulness, to others, 42
holding down a corner, not expressing motivation, 31–32
Holy Spirit
  being in touch with, 38
  infecting us, 42
  missing, 37–38
  not grieving, 14
  prodding of, 36
  teaching all things, 38
Honk, summer theater production of, 9
human beings
  as "a little less than angels," 89
  sinning, 7
humility, 88, 106

I am God's, 67–68
I Had All the Fun Award, 83
instant awareness, of sin, 7
"Is anybody there?" situations, 19

Jane Eyre, musical version of, 7
Jesus Christ
  abiding in, 18
  became one of us, 51
  focusing on when life is going well, 20
  giving up theater for, 3
  as God's Word, 30
  grace of, 48
  as Lord of the universe, 56
  loving us in in poor performance, 69
  meditating on, 63
  needing to BE with, 22
  slapped in play acting, 13
  staying close to, 15–16, 100

Subject Matter Index

talking about naturally, 15–16
turning to during turmoil, 20
use of the name of as an expletive, 66
wanting us to want to be His, 48
judgment, trusting one's own, 11

kindness, to others, 42
King Lear, Lawrence Olivier in, 71
Kingdom of God. *See* God, Kingdom of
Kingdom of Heaven, as like a treasure, 108
knowing God, as an "always" kind of thing, 7

laugh, holding for, 45
law/love banner, for *Godspell*, 57
lead performer, being hard to work with, 97
leaders, 27–28, 77–78, 98
learning and growth, constant state of, 106
life
   becoming unbalanced, 76
   throwing unexpected stuff, 17
lighting changes, 19
lines
   forgetting, 15
   learning from last to first, 61
   speaking on cue, 53
A Lion in Winter, 19
live people in the show, as most important, 92
Lord of my life, Jesus as, 3
Lord of the universe, partying with forever, 48, 84
Lost in Yonkers, playing the grandmother in, 23
love, of God, 67
love and good works, provoking one another to, 42
love and grace of Jesus, being a living witness of, 60
lowly spirit, gaining honor, 106

Macbeth, playing the role of Lennox in, 31
The Madwoman of Chaillot, 33
make-up artist, dreams of becoming, 107
makeup designer, apologizing to, 23
mankind, as a little lower than the angels, 90
meditation, act of, 63
members, of the body, 78
memory, putting God's Word to, 2
Midsummer Night's Dream, dress rehearsal of, 11
mind, relaxing, 63
ministries, suffering, 77–78
mission field, world of the theater as, 45–46
MK (missionary kid), working for medical missionaries in the Amazon basin, 93
moments, of confusion, uncertainty, and doubt as good signs, 49
"The Most Beautiful Thing I've Seen All Day," as a drama club slogan, 89
motivation, for a character, 31, 41, 73
mouth, letting no corrupt speech proceed out of, 30
musical, producing in only thirty hours of rehearsal, 103

Nehemiah, monologues about, 87
"nerves," overcoming, 1
non-Christian friends and acquaintances, seeing us, 92
nonverbal communication, 59

Of Soldiers and Priests, 29
Oliver! 89
Olivier, Laurence, 71–72

performance, working hard on, 91–92
performance-ready, before opening, 47

Subject Matter Index

"performance work" in worship services, 87
performer, well-known, not even trying, 27
Peter, on humbling ourselves, 50
play
  directing one's own, 67
  on an empty stage, 91
playwright, 73, 79, 81
pleasant words, as sweet to the soul, 42
political correctness, as a factor in failure to speak, 53
power, of words, 23, 30
prayer
  in the classroom, 65–66
  importance of, 38
  man of, 37
  not using vain repetitions, 102
  setting before God like incense, 40
pride, 106
production company, as like the body of Christ, 33
professional pursuits, taking over your life, 6
professional theater
  breaking into, 107
  as a tough world, 26
prop "map," making and using, 39–40
the proud, God resisting, 106
proximity, 21
Psalm 23, as meditation matter, 64
public condemnation, 44

quality
  achieving, 103–4
  holding people to, 98
quality theater, 5, 102

real me, being with all people, 86
rehearsal
  angry yelling having no place in, 9
  goal of, 47
  looking forward to, 67
  lots of making quality theater, 102
  not enough, 103
  planning in specific detail, 101
  rehearsing well, to stay close to Jesus, 15–16
relaxation exercises, 63
reputation, as a theater affirming life acknowledging God, 56
respect, confusing fear with, 44
risk, taking big, 25–26
royalty contract, changes violating, 29–30

saved by grace, through faith, 58
script analysis, as a valuable tool, 73–74
Scripture, meditating on, 63
self-evaluation, as an ongoing process, 32
"service to others" attitude, in action, 93
show time, not correctly advertised, 85
sin, 7, 8, 13–14
something is wrong, realizing, 7–8
songs, performing for special occasions, 55
soul, 6, 37, 42, 64
sound operator/stage manager, staying late, 21
speaking the truth in love, as something some of us have to learn, 54
speaking up, in favor of faith, 15
speech
  building others up, 44
  with grace, 42
spiritual giants, 103
spiritual life, 8, 40, 47
spiritual mentors, 11–12
stage combat, 13
stage manager, 21, 39, 41
Starlight Express, as a risk, 26
The Star-Spangled Girl, playing Andy in, 45

Subject Matter Index

students, coming prepared to learn, 105–6
subordinates, dealing with successes of, 77–78
subservience, to those who don't lead well, 28
successes, 77–78
Summer Repertory Theater, forming, 83
supervisors, loving unkind and unloving, 44
"Supper Time," Snoopy's solo song, 1

technical aspects, outshining the cast and crew, 91
television/movie star, as a speaker, 37
tensions, shaking off as a performer, 63
test, classmates helping with, 77
theater
    becoming your whole life, 6
    God calling me out of, 3
    as a group effort, 77
    as intimate, 46
    as a tough profession, 26, 107
    world of, 45
"Theater and Christian Worldview" class, teaching, 5
theater artists
    as horrible human beings, 97
    list of union rules for, 5
    as loads of fun, 83
    motivation for being, 31–32
    never ever "arriving," 106
    practicing daily worship of God, 6
theater arts, Christians in, 45
theater graphics class, test on the color unit, 77
theater money, tithing, 35
theater people, becoming too busy, 76
theater students, arrogant, 105
theater world, challenges to faith everywhere in, 26

theatrical moment, touching us at the core of our being, 87
thoughts and observations, on your spiritual life, 12
The Threepenny Opera, scene change captain for, 43
tithing, theater money, 35
tongue, keeping in check, 10, 24
truth
    adlibbing, 65–66
    hiding in our hearts, 61–62
    speaking in love, 43–44, 54, 66
turmoil, bringing to Christ's feet, 20
tyrant, disliked by cast and crew, 97

the unexpected, Jesus helping with, 18
union rules, for theater artists, 5
Unspoken for Time (Jeff Barker), 79, 81

vignettes, worrying about forgetting the order of, 1
voice, as too sophisticated, 55

walk with Christ
    acting like him, 74
    adlibbing on, 65
    arrogance on, 106
    no formula for, 72
    putting on your walking shoes every day, 108
    rehearsing too much on, 102
    when life is going well, 20
    world of our, 45
weight, trying to lose, 20
"Well done, my good and faithful servant," 79
well-doing, silencing the ignorance of foolish men, 36
"What would Jesus do?" as analysis, 74
Whitman Foundation, 96
wholeness in Christ, 45

Subject Matter Index

wise counsel, trusting and growing
    from, 12
witnessing, God's glory and grace, 92
Word
  became flesh, 52, 60
  of God, 1–2, 62
  hiding in our hearts, 62
words
  making a difference, 29–30
  power of, 23, 30
working, to stay close to the Lord, 21
worship, 5, 6
writers group, reading new plays
    aloud, 55

Yancey, Philip, 50
yelling, 9, 44
You're a Good Man, Charlie Brown,
    1, 55, 83

www.ingramcontent.com/pod-product-compliance
Lightning Source LLC
Chambersburg PA
CBHW030442010526
44118CB00011B/753